AAT

Qualifications and Credit Framework (QCF)

AQ2013

LEVEL 2 CERTIFICATE IN ACCOUNTING

TEXT

Basic Costing

2013 Edition

First edition June 2013
ISBN 9781 4727 0313 2

British Library Cataloguing-in-Publication Data
A catalogue record for this book is available from the British
Library

Published by
BPP Learning Media Ltd
BPP House
Aldine Place
London
W12 8AA

www.bpp.com/learningmedia

Printed in the United Kingdom by Martins of Berwick
Sea View Works
Spittal
Berwick-Upon-Tweed
TD15 1RS

Your learning materials, published by BPP Learning Media Ltd,
are printed on paper sourced from traceable sustainable sources.

CONTENTS

Introduction

A NOTE ABOUT COPYRIGHT

Dear Customer

What does the little © mean and why does it matter?

Your market-leading BPP books, course materials and e-learning materials do not write and update themselves. People write them on their own behalf or as employees of an organisation that invests in this activity. Copyright law protects their livelihoods. It does so by creating rights over the use of the content.

Breach of copyright is a form of theft – as well being a criminal offence in some jurisdictions, it is potentially a serious breach of professional ethics.

With current technology, things might seem a bit hazy but, basically, without the express permission of BPP Learning Media:

- Photocopying our materials is a breach of copyright

- Scanning, ripcasting or conversion of our digital materials into different file formats, uploading them to facebook or emailing them to your friends is a breach of copyright

You can, of course, sell your books, in the form in which you have bought them – once you have finished with them. (Is this fair to your fellow students? We update for a reason). Please note the e-products are sold on a single user licence basis: we do not supply 'unlock' codes to people who have bought them secondhand.

And what about outside the UK? BPP Learning Media strives to make our materials available at prices students can afford by local printing arrangements, pricing policies and partnerships which are clearly listed on our website. A tiny minority ignore this and indulge in criminal activity by illegally photocopying our material or supporting organisations that do. If they act illegally and unethically in one area, can you really trust them?

BPP LEARNING MEDIA'S AAT MATERIALS

The AAT's assessments fall within the **Qualifications and Credit Framework** and most papers are assessed by way of an on demand **computer based assessment**. BPP Learning Media has invested heavily to ensure our materials are as relevant as possible for this method of assessment. In particular, our **suite of online resources** ensures that you are prepared for online testing by allowing you to practise numerous online tasks that are similar to the tasks you will encounter in the AAT's assessments.

Resources

The BPP range of resources comprises:

- **Texts**, covering all the knowledge and understanding needed by students, with numerous illustrations of 'how it works', practical examples and tasks for you to use to consolidate your learning. The majority of tasks within the texts have been written in an interactive style that reflects the style of the online tasks we anticipate the AAT will set. When you purchase a Text you are also granted free access to your Text content online.

- **Question Banks**, including additional learning questions plus the AAT's sample assessment(s) and a number of BPP full practice assessments. Full answers to all questions and assessments, prepared by BPP Learning Media Ltd, are included. Our question banks are provided free of charge in an online environment containing tasks similar to those you will encounter in the AAT's testing environment. This means you can become familiar with being tested in an online environment prior to completing the real assessment.

- **Passcards**, which are handy pocket-sized revision tools designed to fit in a handbag or briefcase to enable you to revise anywhere at any time. All major points are covered in the Passcards which have been designed to assist you in consolidating knowledge.

- **Workbooks**, which have been designed to cover the units that are assessed by way of computer based project/case study. The workbooks contain many practical tasks to assist in the learning process and also a sample assessment or project to work through.

- **Lecturers' resources**, for units assessed by computer based assessments. These provide a further bank of tasks, answers and full practice assessments for classroom use, available separately only to lecturers whose colleges adopt BPP Learning Media material. Adopting colleges will also receive our monthly newsletter.

This Text for Basic Costing has been written specifically to ensure comprehensive yet concise coverage of the AAT's **AQ2013** learning outcomes and assessment criteria.

Each chapter contains:

- Clear, step by step explanation of the topic
- Logical progression and linking from one chapter to the next
- Numerous illustrations of 'how it works'
- Interactive tasks within the text of the chapter itself, with answers at the back of the book. The majority of these tasks have been written in the interactive form that students can expect to see in their real assessments
- Test your learning questions of varying complexity, again with answers supplied at the back of the book. The majority of these questions have been written in the interactive form that students can expect to see in their real assessments

The emphasis in all tasks and test questions is on the practical application of the skills acquired.

Supplements

From time to time we may need to publish supplementary materials to one of our titles. This can be for a variety of reasons, from a small change in the AAT unit guidance to new legislation coming into effect between editions.

You should check our supplements page regularly for anything that may affect your learning materials. All supplements are available free of charge on our supplements page on our website at:

www.bpp.com/about-bpp/aboutBPP/StudentInfo#q4

Customer feedback

If you have any comments about this book, please e-mail ianblackmore@bpp.com or write to Ian Blackmore, AAT Product Manager, BPP Learning Media Ltd, BPP House, Aldine Place, London W12 8AA.

Any feedback we receive is taken into consideration when we periodically update our materials, including comments on style, depth and coverage of AAT standards.

In addition, although our products pass through strict technical checking and quality control processes, unfortunately errors may occasionally slip through when producing material to tight deadlines.

When we learn of an error in a batch of our printed materials, either from internal review processes or from customers using our materials, we want to make sure customers are made aware of this as soon as possible and the appropriate action is taken to minimise the impact on student learning.

As a result, when we become aware of any such errors we will:

(1) Include details of the error and, if necessary, PDF prints of any revised pages under the related subject heading on our 'supplements' page at: www.bpp.com/about-bpp/aboutBPP/StudentInfo#q4

(2) Update the source files ahead of any further printing of the materials

(3) Investigate the reason for the error and take appropriate action to minimise the risk of reoccurrence.

A NOTE ON TERMINOLOGY

The AAT AQ2013 standards and assessments use international terminology based on International Financial Reporting Standards (IFRSs). Although you may be familiar with UK terminology, you need to now know the equivalent international terminology for your assessments.

The following information is taken from an article on the AAT's website and compares IFRS terminology with UK GAAP terminology. It then goes on to describe the impact of IFRS terminology on students studying for each level of the AAT QCF qualification.

Note that since the article containing the information below was published, there have been changes made to some IFRSs. Therefore BPP Learning Media have updated the table and other information below to reflect these changes.

In particular, the primary performance statement under IFRSs which was formerly known as the 'income statement' or the 'statement of comprehensive income' is now called the 'statement of profit or loss' or the 'statement of profit or loss and other comprehensive income'.

What is the impact of IFRS terms on AAT assessments?

The list shown in the table that follows gives the 'translation' between UK GAAP and IFRS.

UK GAAP	IFRS
Final accounts	Financial statements
Trading and profit and loss account	**Statement of profit or loss (or statement of profit or loss and other comprehensive income)**
Turnover or Sales	Revenue or Sales Revenue
Sundry income	Other operating income
Interest payable	Finance costs
Sundry expenses	Other operating costs
Operating profit	Profit from operations
Net profit/loss	Profit/Loss for the year/period
Balance sheet	**Statement of financial position**
Fixed assets	Non-current assets
Net book value	Carrying amount
Tangible assets	Property, plant and equipment

UK GAAP	IFRS
Reducing balance depreciation	Diminishing balance depreciation
Depreciation/Depreciation expense(s)	Depreciation charge(s)
Stocks	Inventories
Trade debtors or Debtors	Trade receivables
Prepayments	Other receivables
Debtors and prepayments	Trade and other receivables
Cash at bank and in hand	Cash and cash equivalents
Trade creditors or Creditors	Trade payables
Accruals	Other payables
Creditors and accruals	Trade and other payables
Long-term liabilities	Non-current liabilities
Capital and reserves	Equity (limited companies)
Profit and loss balance	Retained earnings
Minority interest	Non-controlling interest
Cash flow statement	**Statement of cash flows**

This is certainly not a comprehensive list, which would run to several pages, but it does cover the main terms that you will come across in your studies and assessments. However, you won't need to know all of these in the early stages of your studies – some of the terms will not be used until you reach Level 4. For each level of the AAT qualification, the points to bear in mind are as follows:

Level 2 Certificate in Accounting

The IFRS terms do not impact greatly at this level. Make sure you are familiar with 'receivables' (also referred to as 'trade receivables'), 'payables' (also referred to as 'trade payables'), and 'inventories'. The terms sales ledger and purchases ledger – together with their control accounts – will continue to be used. Sometimes the control accounts might be called 'trade receivables control account' and 'trade payables control account'. The other term to be aware of is 'non-current asset' – this may be used in some assessments.

Level 3 Diploma in Accounting

At this level you need to be familiar with the term 'financial statements'. The financial statements comprise a 'statement of profit or loss' (previously known as an income statement), and a 'statement of financial position'. In the statement of profit or loss the term 'revenue' or 'sales revenue' takes the place of 'sales', and 'profit for the year' replaces 'net profit'. Other terms may be used in the statement of financial position – eg 'non-current assets' and 'carrying amount'. However, specialist limited company terms are not required at this level.

Level 4 Diploma in Accounting

At Level 4 a wider range of IFRS terms is needed, and in the case of Financial statements, are already in use – particularly those relating to limited companies. Note especially that a statement of profit or loss becomes a 'statement of profit or loss and other comprehensive income'.

Note: The information above was taken from an AAT article from the 'assessment news' area of the AAT website (www.aat.org.uk). However, it has been adapted by BPP Learning Media for changes in international terminology since the article was published and for any changes needed to reflect the move from AQ2010 to AQ2013.

ASSESSMENT STRATEGY

Basic Costing is an introduction to costing at level 2 which recognises the need to build a sound foundation in costing giving the student the relevant knowledge and skills to take forward to the more complex Costing and Management Accounting that will be studied at levels 3 and 4.

The assessment is normally a two hour computer based assessment. It comprises 17 tasks.

The level descriptor below describes the ability and skills students at this level must demonstrate to achieve competence.

QCF Level descriptor	Summary
	Achievement at level 2 reflects the ability to select and use relevant knowledge, ideas, skills and procedures to complete well-defined tasks and address straightforward problems. It includes taking responsibility for completing tasks and procedures and exercising autonomy and judgement subject to overall direction or guidance.
	Knowledge and understanding
	▪ Use understanding of facts, procedures and ideas to complete well-defined tasks and address straight-forward problems
	▪ Interpret relevant information and ideas
	▪ Be aware of the types of information that are relevant to the area of study or work
	Application and action
	▪ Complete well-defined, generally routine tasks and address straightforward problems
	▪ Select and use relevant skills and procedures
	▪ Identify, gather and use relevant information to inform actions
	▪ Identify how effective actions have been
	Autonomy and accountability
	▪ Take responsibility for completing tasks and procedures
	▪ Exercise autonomy and judgement subject to overall direction or guidance

Task	Learning outcome	Assessment criteria	Max marks	Title for topics within task range
1	1	1.2, 1.3	8	Costing and accounting systems
2	1,2	1.1 1.2 1.3 2.1	8	Classification of cost by element Classification of cost by nature
3	1,2	1.1 1.2 1.3 2.1	8	Classification of cost by function and/or behaviour
4	1,2	1.5 2.2 2.3	6	Coding to cost, profit and investment centres using a numeric coding system
5	1,2	1.5 2.2 2.3	6	Coding to cost, profit and investment centres using an alpha numeric system
6	2	2.7	9	Classification of fixed, variable and semi-variable costs
7	2	2.1 2.8	8	Classify overheads
8	2	2.4	14	Identify different types of inventory using a manufacturing account
9	2	2.5	9	Identify methods of issue and inventory valuation
10	2	2.5	9	Calculate inventory valuations and issues of inventory
11	2	2.6	8	Definition of labour payment by method/Calculation of pay using time-rate and overtime
12	2	2.6	8	Calculation of pay using piecework

Task	Learning outcome	Assessment criteria	Max marks	Title for topics within task range
13	2	2.6	9	Calculation of pay using bonus
14	1,3	1.4 1.5 3.1 3.4 3.5	12	Spreadsheet exercise entering income and expenditure (product cost, cost behaviour table) and formatting
15	3	3.2	8	Use of spreadsheets to present information and facilitate internal reporting
16	1,3	1.4 1.5 3.3 3.4 3.5	12	Spreadsheet exercise reorganising budgeted and actual data on income and expenditure
17	3	3.5	8	Formatting exercise reorganising data and Identifying significant variance differences

AAT UNIT GUIDE

Basic Costing (BCST)

Introduction

Please read this document in conjunction with the standards for the unit Basic Costing.

The purpose of the unit

The purpose of the Basic Costing unit is to give students a basic introduction to costing at Level 2, recognising the need to build a sound foundation in costing to give the candidate the relevant knowledge and skills to take forward to the more complex costing and management accounting units they will study at Levels 3 and 4.

At the same time students are made aware of the importance of the costing system as a source of information for internal management decision making as contrasted against financial accounting, which looks outwards. Students need to understand what constitutes cost in different organisations. For instance a cost structure within a manufacturing industry will be different from a cost structure within a service industry and as a consequence the costing systems will differ.

Another learning outcome recognises the importance of spreadsheets as a means of communicating costing information. The assessment will test students' understanding of spreadsheets as a method of conveying costing information, the important phrase here being conveying costing information. It must be stressed that students are not being assessed on their spreadsheet ability, but on their basic understanding of spreadsheets as a method of presenting costing information. The assessment will be a mixture of simulation to test skill, and knowledge based tasks to test understanding. It will be assumed that student's will have had exposure to spreadsheets as a method of presenting information in preparation for this assessment.

Learning objectives

The Basic Costing unit requires students to have an underlying knowledge and understanding of the nature of a cost accounting system within an organisation and its component parts as well as an understanding of how it operates. Students will also be required to demonstrate the skills they have acquired in using the cost system to record or extract data and providing information on actual and expected costs using a simulated spreadsheet format.

It should be stressed that the unit is looking to provide an introduction to costing and to develop basic skills that students will build upon in later studies.

Learning outcomes

In total there are three learning outcomes that are broken down into assessment criteria. The learning outcomes are:

(1) Understand the cost recording system within an organisation

(2) Be able to use the cost recording system to record or extract data

(3) Be able to use spreadsheets to provide information on actual and budgeted income and expenditure.

The assessment will cover all of the learning outcomes and assessment criteria of the QCF unit Basic Costing.

Learning Outcome	Assessment Criteria	Covered in Chapter
Understand the cost recording system within an organisation	Explain the nature of an organisation's business transactions in relation to its accounting systems	1
	Explain the purpose and structure of a costing system within an organisation	
	Identify the relationships between the costing and accounting systems within the organisation	
	Identify sources of income and expenditure information for historic, current and forecast periods	
	Identify types of cost, profit and investment centres	3
Be able to use the cost recording system to record or extract data	Explain how materials, labour and expenses are classified and recorded	2
	Explain different methods of coding data	6
	Classify and code cost information for materials, labour and expenses	2,6
	Classify different types of inventory as: raw materials, part-finished goods (work-in-progress), finished goods	4
	Calculate inventory valuations and issues using these methods: First In First Out (FIFO), Last In First Out (LIFO), Weighted Average	4
	Use these methods to calculate payments for labour: Time-rate, Piecework rate, Bonuses	5

Learning Outcome	Assessment Criteria	Covered in Chapter
	Explain the nature of expenses and distinguish between fixed, variable and semi-variable overheads	3
	Calculate the direct cost of a product or service	3,4
Be able to use spreadsheets to provide information on actual and budgeted income and expenditure	Enter income and expenditure data into a spreadsheet	7
	Explain how spreadsheets can be used to present information on income and expenditure and to facilitate internal reporting	
	Enter budgeted and actual data on income and expenditure into a spreadsheet to provide a comparison of the results and identify differences	
	Use basic spreadsheet functions and formulas	
	Format the spreadsheet to present data in a clear and unambiguous manner and in accordance with organisational requirements	

Delivery guidance: Basic Principles of Costing (Knowledge)

1. **Demonstrate an understanding of the cost recording system within an organisation**

    1.1K Explain the nature of an organisation's business transactions in relation to its accounting systems

    Students need to understand what constitutes cost in different organisations. For instance, a cost structure within a manufacturing industry will be different from a cost structure within a service industry and as a consequence the costing systems will differ. Students will be required to identify the elements of cost (materials, labour, and expenses/overheads) within an organisation and the nature of the cost (direct or indirect), which will be assessed by two tasks in the assessment

1.2K   Explain the purpose and structure of a costing system within an organisation

Students must develop an understanding of what a costing system brings to an organisation. In order to do this they must be able to classify cost by element, nature and behaviour (fixed, variable or semi-variable). From this students must be able to explain the purpose and role of the costing system, in particular determining product cost and hence selling price, valuing inventory, providing information for financial statements and management decision making. The assessment for this criterion will be through one task testing understanding of a costing system and what it brings to an organisation

1.3K   Identify the relationships between the costing and accounting systems within the organisation

Students must understand the nature of the costing and accounting systems within the organisation. This requires knowledge of their purpose and what they are trying to achieve. Essential to this is the need to understand how each system uses cost; the costing system dependent upon the information that is required for it (product cost will need cost classified by element) contrasted with the accounting system which will require cost classified by function (production, administration, selling and distribution, finance etc). Assessment testing differences between costing and accounting systems will be explicit to one task and the use of cost will be explicit to two tasks

1.4K   Identify sources of income and expenditure information for historic, current and forecast periods

Students must be able to identify how financial accounts are used to provide data for historic periods, how actual or estimated materials and labour and estimated overheads are used, for instance, to arrive at a job cost (current period), and how standard and budgeted costs are used for forecast periods. This criterion will be implicitly assessed over a number of tasks throughout the assessment

1.5K   Identify types of cost, profit and investment centres

Students will be expected to identify what is meant by a cost centre, a profit centre and an investment centre, why they are used in a costing system and be able to classify a given centre appropriately. Such knowledge will be assessed explicitly through the two coding tasks and implicitly in tasks related to learning outcome 3

2. Be able to use the cost recording system to record or extract data

2.1K   Explain how materials, labour and expenses are classified and recorded. Students must be able to classify and record across a range of business organisations' material, labour and expenses as direct or indirect; fixed or variable. Assessment will be across a range of tasks covering the elements of cost, materials, labour and expenses/overheads. Note that, for this unit, expenses are interpreted as overheads and throughout the guidance and ensuing assessments the terms expenses and overheads are interchangeable. It is acknowledged there is a category of expense termed direct expenses however such a classification is beyond the scope of this unit. For assessment purposes, expenses will be known as overheads and will always be indirect in nature.

2.2K   Explain different methods of coding data

Students must be able to explain and understand a range of coding systems (numeric, alphabetic, alpha-numeric). Students' understanding will be assessed through two coding tasks in the assessment.

2.3S   Classify and code cost information for materials, labour and expenses

Students will be assessed on their ability to code materials, labour and expenses/overheads using numeric and alpha-numeric systems of coding over two tasks

2.4K   Classify different types of inventory as: raw materials, part-finished goods (work-in-progress), finished goods

Students must understand the flow of inventory through the stages of manufacture and be able to identify the components of a cost statement for manufactured goods, appreciating the classification of inventory in arriving at direct materials used, direct cost, factory cost of goods manufactured and cost of goods sold. Students will be required to calculate sub-totals and the total of the cost statement

2.5S   Calculate inventory valuations and issues of inventory using these methods: First in first out (FIFO, Last in first out (LIFO), Weighted average

Students must be able to use FIFO, LIFO and Weighted average (AVCO) as methods of costing issues of inventories from stores and valuing closing inventories. Assessment will be over two tasks. The first will require students to determine method from data given and the second will require students to calculate the cost of one issue and value of closing inventory for each method

2.6S Use these methods to calculate payments for labour: Time-rate, Piecework rate, Bonuses

Students will be required to understand the methods of payment for labour in order to calculate payments. Note that time-rate will include calculation of an overtime time-rate. Assessment will be over three tasks that will test ability to identify a payment method and calculate pay using each method. Students will not be required to have knowledge of specific bonus schemes.

2.7K Explain the nature of expenses and distinguish between fixed, variable and semi-variable overheads

Students will be expected to define what expenses/overheads are and then classify their behaviour as fixed, variable or semi-variable. A cost behaviour task will also require students to demonstrate their understanding by showing how costs including overheads behave with changes in the level of output.

2.8S Calculate the direct cost of a product or service

Students will be assessed over two tasks. Although a new assessment criterion this was assessed implicitly before. For future assessments students will be expected to identify direct (prime) cost in a manufacturing account in one task and build up a product cost with the identification of direct cost and total cost

3. **Be able to use spreadsheets to provide information on actual and budgeted income and expenditure**

3.1S Enter income and expenditure data into a spreadsheet

The task for this assessment criterion could be a range of product costs or a range of outputs. The data will be set out in a simulated spreadsheet. Students will be expected to format the spreadsheet by completing headers and will also be expected to demonstrate their costing skills by completing the table data. As supplementary students will be expected to identify or state formulas for totals and other calculations.

3.2K Explain how spreadsheets can be used to present information on income and expenditure and to facilitate internal reporting

Students will be expected to demonstrate their understanding of how spreadsheets can be used to present information through knowledge based tasks that will require students to select the correct statement or recognise it as being true or false

3.3S Enter budgeted and actual data on income and expenditure into a spreadsheet to provide a comparison of the results and identify differences

Students will be expected to understand basic budgeting and the concepts budgeted cost, actual cost, budgeted income, actual income and budgeted profit. Students will also be expected to understand the basic variances arising from the above comparisons and recognise them as being either favourable or adverse. It must be stressed that the analysis will be at a basic level and no understanding of sub-variances will be required. Students will be presented with a simulated spreadsheet and they will be expected to complete headings and complete data entry using their costing skills to do so. Students will be expected to identify or state formulas for totals and other calculations

3.4S Use basic spreadsheet functions and formulas

Students will be expected to complete headings and totals for two simulated spreadsheets and will be expected to add, subtract, multiply, divide and total and recognise formulas for such. A separate task will see students presented with a set of budgeted data and variances and they could be asked to reorder, average or express as %

3.5S Format the spreadsheet to present data in a clear and unambiguous manner and in accordance with organisational requirements

Students will be expected to format a spreadsheet by reorganising data using functions such as ascending, descending, auto sum etc. They will be expected to present significant variances in a clear and unambiguous manner to managers

chapter 1:
INTRODUCTION TO BASIC COSTING SYSTEMS

chapter coverage 📖

This opening chapter of the Text introduces you to the world of business. You will read about costing systems and how these record the activities of the business. The chapter is written for someone who is new to business so if you are already familiar with these topics, use this chapter to refresh your memory. The topics covered are:

- ✎ Types of business. An introduction to the different types of business organisation

- ✎ Types of transaction. The nature of the transactions that businesses have and ways of classifying them

- ✎ Types of industry. The different types of industry or business environment that you may have to deal with

- ✎ Types of accounting system. The manual and computerised accounting systems used in business

- ✎ The purpose of accounting. This explains how the transactions you record lead into the ultimate outputs which are statements for owners and others to see how the business has performed

- ✎ Management information. The purpose and structure of a costing system within an organisation

- ✎ Relationship between financial and management accounting. The relationship between the costing and accounting systems in the organisation

- ✎ Types of comparison. The sources of income and expenditure information for historic, current and forecast periods

TYPES OF BUSINESS

A business can be set up in a variety of different ways depending upon its nature, its size and its organisation.

Sole trader

The simplest type of business is that of a SOLE TRADER. A sole trader is someone who trades under their own name. Many businesses are sole traders, from electricians through to accountants. Being a sole trader does not mean that the owner is the only person working in the business. Some sole traders are the only person in the business but many will also employ a number of other staff. Even so, in most cases the owner will be in charge of most business functions, such as buying and selling the goods or services, doing the bookkeeping and producing accounts. In some instances, however, the sole trader will employ an external bookkeeper, who may also be a sole trader, in order to update the accounting records regularly.

The owner of the business is the one who contributes the capital to the business, although it might also have loans, either commercial or from friends. The owner is also the only party to benefit from the profits of the business and this will normally be done by the owner taking money or goods out of the business, known as DRAWINGS.

Partnership

A PARTNERSHIP is a group of individuals who are trading together with the intention of making a profit. Partnerships are often created as a sole trader's business expands and more capital and expertise are needed within the business. Typical partnerships are those of accountants, solicitors and dentists and usually comprise between two and about 20 partners. As partnerships tend to be larger than sole traders there will usually be more employees and a greater likelihood of a bookkeeper being employed to maintain the accounting records.

Each of the partners will contribute capital to the business and will normally take part in the business activities. The profits of the business will be shared between the partners and this is normally done by setting up a partnership agreement where the financial rights of each partner are set out. Just as with sole traders, the partners will withdraw part of the profits that are due to them in the form of drawings from the business although, in some cases, partners may also be paid a salary by the business.

Limited company

Most larger businesses will be formed as LIMITED COMPANIES. A limited company is where the owners of the business own the company's shares as SHAREHOLDERS but the business is often managed by a completely different set of people, the directors. In legal terms a limited company is a completely separate entity from the owners, the shareholders. Many companies are run as private limited companies (whose names end in 'Ltd') and often the shareholders and the directors are the same people. The largest companies, however, are public limited companies (whose names end in 'plc') and in these companies the shareholders and the directors are usually completely different. The directors run the company on behalf of the shareholders, the owners, and are accountable to the shareholders for their management of the business and how they manage its assets (their 'stewardship').

The shareholders provide the capital for the business by buying shares in the company, and they share in the profits of the company by being paid DIVIDENDS. The accounting records that are required for a limited company are regulated by law and many companies have a large and comprehensive accounting function.

Limited liability

The main difference between the trading of a sole trader and a partnership on the one hand and a limited company on the other is the concept of limited liability. If the business of a sole trader or a partnership runs out of money and is declared bankrupt then the sole trader or partners are personally liable for any outstanding debts of the business. However, the shareholders of a company have limited liability which means that once they have fully paid for their shares they cannot be called upon for any more money if the company runs out and is declared insolvent. All that they will lose is the amount that they have paid for their shares.

TYPES OF TRANSACTION

Whether a business is run as a sole trader, partnership or company it will still carry out all of the same types of business transaction, although on different scales.

Typical transactions that businesses undertake include the following:

- Buying materials to make goods
- Making goods
- Selling goods or services

- Buying goods to resell

- Paying expenses

- Paying wages

- Buying items like furniture, vans or a building (known as non-current assets) for use in the business in the long term

- Paying money into the bank

- Withdrawing cash from the bank

- Paying the owners (either as drawings or dividends)

- Paying taxes such as VAT

It is vital that each and every one of these transactions is correctly recorded in the accounting records of the business and much of this is what will be covered in your studies.

As well as recording the everyday transactions, the accounting records also provide valuable information to the owners or managers of the business. The records should indicate:

- how much money is owed by the business and to whom
- how much money is owing to the business and from whom
- what non-current assets the business has
- how much inventory the business holds

Again, if the business is to run efficiently the accounting records must be capable of providing accurate information on all of these areas.

There are two important distinctions that must be made between the types of transaction of a business. These are between cash and credit transactions and between capital and revenue transactions.

CASH TRANSACTIONS occur where payment is made or received immediately. A cash transaction is not limited to payments and receipts made in notes and coins, as they are also made by cheque, debit card or automated payment. The important factor is the timing of the payment.

CREDIT TRANSACTIONS by contrast are transactions in which the goods or services are given or received now but it is agreed that payment is to be made or received at a future date. This will normally involve the issue or receipt of an invoice and the creation of a TRADE RECEIVABLE (the person who owes the business money ie the credit customer) or a TRADE PAYABLE (the person to whom the business owes money ie the credit supplier).

Task 1

(a)   A sale is made for £100 and it is agreed that this will be paid for in cash in two weeks' time. Is this a cash transaction or a credit transaction? Tick the correct box in the table below.

(b)   A new car is purchased for use in the business and is paid for at the time of the purchase by cheque. Is this a cash or credit transaction? Tick the correct box in the table below.

Transaction	Cash	Credit
Sale for £100		
Purchase of car		

CAPITAL TRANSACTIONS are the purchase and sale of items that are to be used in the business for a considerable period of time rather than being purchased for immediate use or resale. This might include the purchase of buildings, machinery, office furniture or motor vehicles. These NON-CURRENT ASSETS of the business can be purchased either for cash or more usually on credit. Capital transactions should not be confused with the initial capital that the owners of a business pay into the business.

REVENUE TRANSACTIONS are the everyday income and expenses of the business. These will include sales, the purchase of goods for resale, the general running expenses of the business and the payment of wages. Again, these transactions can either be for cash or on credit.

TYPES OF INDUSTRY

We have been talking in general terms about the types of transaction that a business undertakes. You should be aware, however, that there are many different types of business operating in varying types of industry and each will have very different types of transaction. For the purposes of this unit there are three types of industry or business environment that you are likely to have to deal with.

MANUFACTURING ORGANISATIONS are businesses which actually make the goods that they sell on to other businesses. Therefore such organisations tend to buy the raw materials that are necessary in order to produce the goods and then pay the wages of the employees who make these goods.

RETAIL ORGANISATIONS buy in goods made by a manufacturer in order to sell on to the final customer. Such organisations buy finished goods rather than raw materials and pay the wages of the shop assistants who sell the goods to

customers. Many retail organisations have high property costs as they need to purchase or rent the buildings in which to house the shops.

SERVICE ORGANISATIONS are businesses that do not manufacture or sell a physical product but instead provide a service, such as accountants or a transport company. Such organisations tend not to buy many physical goods but they have high wages and salaries costs and expenses.

TYPES OF ACCOUNTING SYSTEM

As you will be starting to realise, business life is complicated and all businesses, of whatever size or form, will need an accounting system that is capable of accurately recording all the transactions of the business and periodically producing a picture of what the business owns and owes. Without such an accounting system the owners would not know how the business was doing nor be able to keep track of payments that need to be made and receipts that should be received.

Most businesses, unless they are very small, will have an accounting system that is based upon double entry book-keeping methods. These are considered in detail in the Processing Book-keeping Transactions (PBKT) and Control Accounts Journals and the Banking System (CJBS) units. In general terms, however, the accounting system must be capable of recording each of the transactions made and categorising them as the correct type of transaction such as sales, purchases, telephone expense etc. The accounting system may be manual or computerised, or it may be a mixture of the two.

Manual accounting systems are where the accounting records are maintained by hand and are written-up by the book-keeper or the accounts department staff. Although totally manual accounting systems are becoming increasingly rare as they have been replaced by computerised accounting packages and PCs, most of the material in this unit will be assessed based on a manual system as this is the best method of testing your competence.

This unit will however introduce you to some of the uses of basic spreadsheets in a business. Spreadsheets are available to anyone who has access to even a very basic PC, and so are often used in very small, simple businesses where a computerised accounting package is not necessary. We shall see in the final chapters of this text that a spreadsheet can be used to monitor what is actually happening in the business against what we hoped would happen. It can also be used to produce some clear, easily understandable information on which to base decisions.

You will learn about using a PC with an accounting software package to record all transactions and produce basic accounting reports in the Computerised Accounting (CPAG) unit.

THE PURPOSE OF ACCOUNTING

As we have seen the purpose of accounting is to record and classify accurately the transactions of the business. The end product of this recording and classification is that, at intervals, financial statements for the business can be drawn up. For a company these financial statements are required by law but sole traders and partnerships will also usually wish to draw them up in order to assess the success and management of the business.

The two main financial statements are the STATEMENT OF PROFIT OR LOSS and the STATEMENT OF FINANCIAL POSITION. Although the preparation of these statements is not covered in level 2 AAT studies, we will look briefly at them now to gain a better insight into the nature of financial accounting as opposed to management accounting.

Statement of profit or loss

INCOME less EXPENSES = PROFIT or LOSS

The statement of profit or loss shows how the business has performed during the last accounting period, typically six months or a year. It summarises all of the income of the business, including sales revenue and other operating income such as rent receivable, and deducts all of the expenses. The expenses will include the cost of goods that have been purchased for resale, the cost of making any goods for sale, the costs of employing any staff and all of the other everyday costs of running the business.

If the income is greater than the expenses a profit has been made, but if expenses exceed income then a loss has occurred.

Statement of financial position

The statement of financial position is a list of the monetary values of all of the ASSETS, LIABILITIES and CAPITAL of the business on the last day of the accounting period. Assets are amounts that the business owns and liabilities are amounts that the business owes. This is shown in the accounting equation, which you study in Processing Bookkeeping Transactions (PBKT):

ASSETS minus LIABILITIES = CAPITAL

We have already seen that the non-current assets of a business are those assets that are held for long-term use in the business. There are also CURRENT ASSETS, which are the shorter-term assets of the business. These will include the INVENTORY of the business, which are materials or goods that are due to be used in manufacture or just sold but that have not yet been used or sold. There will also be trade receivables of the business, which are amounts that are owed to

the business, usually by customers to whom credit sales have been made. It will also include any cash or bank balances that the business may have.

The liabilities of the business will include payables, which are the amounts that the business owes to other parties. These could be trade payables to whom money is owed for goods that have been purchased on credit, but also other payables in respect of money owed for wages, short-term loans that are outstanding or amounts owed to the tax authorities. An overdraft at the bank is also a liability.

The total of the assets minus the liabilities is the capital of the business. Capital is made up of the initial amount that the owner or owners paid into the business plus any accumulated profits of the business minus any drawings or dividends that the owners have taken. This is the amount that is effectively owed back to the owner.

For the purposes of this unit you do not need to prepare financial statements for publication externally but it is useful to be aware at this stage of the final product of all of the accounting that you will be doing in your AAT studies.

MANAGEMENT INFORMATION

The FINANCIAL ACCOUNTING SYSTEM of the business provides the information necessary to prepare financial statements for the business at the end of each accounting period, normally a year. In these costs are classified by their function, that is production, selling and distribution, administration, and finance. We explain this later in the chapter when we look at the relationship between the financial accounting system and the system below.

The managers of the business require other financial information on a more regular basis in order to run it efficiently on a day-to-day basis. This is provided by the MANAGEMENT ACCOUNTING SYSTEM which classifies costs by element so that the cost of producing any unit of product is broken down into material, labour and overheads. The system collects similar costs together for management accounting purposes so that they can be further analysed.

The role of management

The management of a business must ensure that the business is run as well and efficiently as possible. There are three main elements involved in this:

- Decision-making
- Planning
- Control

Decision-making

The managers of a business constantly make decisions about how the business is operated. These will range from long-term strategic decisions through to short-term, day-to-day decisions.

Here are a few examples of the types of long-term decisions that may be made:

- Which markets to operate in – the UK, Europe, or worldwide

- How to organise the business – on a centralised basis or as a series of divisions

- Where to locate factories, warehouses etc

- How many employees to have and in what locations

- Whether or not to expand the business

Other decisions may be classed as medium-term decisions:

- Whether to finance the business by taking out a further loan
- How to advertise and market the products
- Which products to continue making and which to discontinue, if any

Yet more decisions will be of a short-term nature:

- How many raw materials or goods for resale to buy
- Which suppliers to use
- How much overtime work is required
- Whether to rent more warehouse space
- How many products to produce

As you can see there are many aspects to the DECISION-MAKING role of management, and in order to make informed decisions managers require detailed, relevant and up-to-date information.

HOW IT WORKS

If the managers of a manufacturing organisation are trying to decide which products to continue to produce for the following year, they will need information about each type of product:

- What does each product cost to make?
- How much is each product sold for?
- How many of each product are sold?
- How many hours does each product require for manufacture?
- How much profit does each product make?

This type of information is not available from the financial accounting records. Although, for example, all of the purchases of raw materials are recorded in a

purchases account in the general ledger, they are not split into which products they are used to manufacture. This is the purpose of management accounting – to provide the type of detailed cost and income information that managers require.

Planning

If a business is to operate efficiently then there is a great deal of forward planning required. In a similar manner to the decisions that have to be made, these plans will range from long-term strategic plans to much shorter-term operational plans.

The long-term strategy of the business will include plans for the markets where the products are to be sold, the development and improvement of products, and the expansion or contraction plans of the business.

In the shorter term the plans that must be made for a manufacturing business will include:

- How many products to produce
- What materials are required for this production and what they will cost
- How many employees are required for production and how much will they be paid
- How many machines are required for production
- What the advertising costs will be
- What the administration costs will be

These plans are produced as financial estimates of the future or BUDGETS. You will examine budgets in detail in your later studies so we just consider the briefest details here, in the context of a manufacturing business. In the final chapter of the text we shall look at how spreadsheets can assist in the production and use of budgets.

Budgets are normally produced for the next year ahead. The budget process usually starts with determining the demand for each product in that year and, therefore, the number of products to be produced. Then there will be a variety of budgets produced, some in terms of number of products or hours to be worked and some in terms of costs and income. Typical budgets may include:

- Sales revenue budget – the number and price of the products expected to be sold
- A production budget – number of products to be produced, amount of raw materials required and the cost of these
- A labour budget – number of employee hours required for production and the cost of these

- Production expenses budget – cost of the expenses involved in manufacturing the products

- Selling and administration costs budget – the selling and administration costs necessary to support production and sales

- Finance cost budget – how much it will cost to finance the business's operations in terms of interest on loans and overdrafts

All these budgets are required to ensure that the business runs efficiently, that there are enough materials for production and sufficient numbers of employees to make the products.

Control

When the decisions for a business have been made and the plans drafted as an overall budget, managers must ensure that these plans are followed and that the decisions taken are the correct ones. To do this they must have control over all aspects of the business.

The system of control usually works by regular comparison of the actual production, sales and costs of the business to the budget. In practice, there are likely to be differences between what actually happens and what was planned in the budget, and these differences are known as VARIANCES.

In order to control the business, managers require regular updates to be made aware of any significant variances from the budgeted figures. Armed with this information they may change the plans or make different decisions. Therefore it is important that these variances are accurately reported on a regular basis. We shall see in the final chapter of this text how spreadsheets can assist with this task as well.

Task 2

Management has to ensure that the business is run as well and efficiently as possible. There are three main elements to this. Tick the three relevant correct boxes in the table below.

Activity	Yes
Analysing variances	
Decision-making	
Planning	
Selling goods and services	
Control	

RELATIONSHIP BETWEEN FINANCIAL AND MANAGEMENT ACCOUNTING

The managers of a business need particular types of information about its activities to plan, make decisions and control the business. This information cannot always be taken from the financial accounting records.

It is important to realise, however, that the information required comes from the same source as the information used for financial accounting, namely the recording of the business's transactions. It is simply classified and collected in a different manner.

In our example here we refer to some of the day books and ledger accounts covered in PBKT and CJBS. Bear with us if you haven't studied those units yet. The examples are here to show you how data collected for financial accounting is also used by managers in their day-to-day running of the business, or management accounting.

HOW IT WORKS

A batch of purchase invoices from credit suppliers is received by a manufacturing business. They are entered into the purchases day book and referenced to the correct credit supplier. The totals of the purchases day book are posted to the general ledger accounts and the individual invoices are posted to the individual supplier accounts in the purchases ledger. This is all done within the financial accounting system.

However, the information from the purchase invoices is also recorded for management accounting purposes. Each invoice is analysed to determine whether it is for materials or expenses and what part of the business it relates to, such as production, administration etc (known as 'cost centres', a term we shall come back to). The cost of the purchase or expense (net of VAT) is added to the costs already collected for that cost centre. This takes place in the management accounting records.

In the financial accounting system we are concerned with:

- The fact that these are purchases on credit
- Which credit supplier the invoice is from
- Getting the invoice paid

In the management accounting system we are concerned with:

- The type of cost represented by each purpose
- The cost centre the cost relates to

TYPES OF COMPARISON

Earlier, we considered the role of management in a business and that one of the key elements of this role is control. One way in which the costs and income of a business can be controlled is by comparing actual figures to either an earlier period's figures or budgeted figures.

For this unit only one comparison is required: between expected (budgeted or standard) figures and actual figures. We work through this, using spreadsheets, in the final chapter, which will bring together all of the topics we learn in this unit.

CHAPTER OVERVIEW

- There are three main types of business – a sole trader, a partnership or a limited company.

- Many transactions are undertaken by a business and these can be categorised as cash or credit transactions and as capital or revenue transactions.

- Different types of business will have predominantly different types of transactions – the types of industry that you may have to deal with are manufacturing, retail and service organisations.

- Accounting systems can be manual or computerised or a combination of the two, and may make use of spreadsheets.

- Management has three main roles in an organisation – decision-making, planning and control – and relevant, up-to-date information is required in order to carry out these roles.

- Decision-making covers long-term strategic decisions, medium-term decisions and short-term, day-to-day decisions.

- Planning is also both long range and shorter range –plans for the next year are set out in budgets which can be in terms of physical resources that are expected to be required, and in financial terms.

- Control is where the actual results of the business are compared to the budgeted figures and significant variances are reported to management.

- Businesses tend to be split up into cost centres for management accounting purposes and the costs of each cost centre are collected together.

Keywords

Sole trader – a business that is run by an individual trading under their own name

Drawings – amounts taken out of the business by the owner

Partnership – a business run by a number of individuals trading together with the intention of making a profit

Limited company – a business that is owned by the shareholders and run by the directors – the owners have limited liability

Shareholders – the people who own shares in a limited company

Dividends – payments taken by shareholders out of a limited company's profits

Cash transactions – transactions whereby payment or receipt is immediate

Credit transactions – transactions whereby payment or receipt is to be made at some future date

Capital transactions – purchases of assets for long-term use in the business, and gains from sales of these assets

Non-current assets – assets purchased for long-term use in the business

Revenue transactions – all other day-to-day revenue and expenses

Receivable – someone who owes money to the business

Payable – someone to whom the business owes money

Manufacturing organisation – a business that makes the goods that it is to sell

Retail organisation – a business that buys in ready-made goods in order to sell to customers

Service organisation – a business that provides a service rather than a physical product

Statement of profit or loss – financial accounting statement showing sales revenue plus other operating income less expenses equalling a profit or a loss

Statement of financial position – financial accounting statement showing the assets, liabilities and capital of the business on a particular date

Assets – amounts that the business owns

Liabilities – amounts that the business owes

Capital – amount that the business owes its owner once liabilities are deducted from assets

Keywords cont'd

Current assets – short-term assets of the business

Inventory – raw materials, items manufactured for sales and goods purchased for eventual resale but as yet unsold

Financial accounting system – the recording of the business' transactions in the general and subsidiary ledgers in order to prepare financial statements: the statement of profit or loss and the statement of financial position.

Management accounting system – the recording of the business' transactions in order to provide useful information for management

Decision-making – the management role of making both long- and short-term decisions regarding the operations of the business

Budgets – the plans of the business for the next year set out in terms of resources required or in monetary terms

Variances – the differences that arise when the actual results of the business differ from the budgeted results

TEST YOUR LEARNING

Test 1

For each of the following transactions indicate whether it should be classified as a cash or credit transaction. Tick the correct box.

	Cash	Credit
Purchase of a van with payment agreed in one month		
Sale of goods paid for by credit card		
Purchase of printer paper accompanied by an invoice		
Sale of goods paid for by cheque		
Purchase of printer paper by cheque		

Test 2

For each of the following transactions indicate whether it should be classified as a capital or revenue transaction. Tick the correct box.

	Capital	Revenue
Purchase of a computer for resale to a customer by a computer retailer		
Purchase of a computer by a computer retailer for use in the sales office		
Payment of wages by an accounting firm		
Purchase of a building by a property developer to serve as head office		

Test 3

In the table below, tick three items that would appear in a statement of profit or loss and two that would appear in a statement of financial position.

	Statement of profit or loss	Statement of financial position
Sales revenue		
Non-current assets		
Expenses		
Current assets		
Profit or loss		

Test 4

The table below lists some of the characteristics of financial accounting and management accounting systems.

Indicate two characteristics for each system by putting a tick in the relevant column of the table below.

Characteristic	Financial accounting	Management accounting
It helps with decision-making within the business		
Its end-product consists of statements for external publication		
It focuses on costs		
It focuses on asset valuations		

chapter 2:
ELEMENTS OF COST

---

chapter coverage 📖

In this chapter we consider the manner in which costs are analysed and classified for management accounting purposes and the different types of cost that an organisation will incur. The topics covered are:

- ✍ Classification of costs
- ✍ Capital and revenue expenditure
- ✍ Classification of costs by function
- ✍ Direct and indirect cost elements
- ✍ Identifying cost centres
- ✍ Materials. Analysing materials costs
- ✍ Labour. The elements that make up gross pay and basic pay
- ✍ Overtime
- ✍ Bonus payments
- ✍ Employer's NIC contribution
- ✍ Expenses/overheads. Specific expenses and joint expenses
- ✍ Service organisations

CLASSIFICATION OF COSTS

In the financial accounting system costs are classified as:

- Purchases
- Wages
- Various expenses – rent, telephone, electricity etc

In the management accounting system the classification of costs is rather more detailed, as the information required by management is more detailed. The basic classification of costs is between the ELEMENTS OF COST: materials, labour and expenses. However, for management accounting purposes, the costs need to be analysed further.

CAPITAL AND REVENUE EXPENDITURE

The expenses of a business can be categorised as either capital or revenue. We looked at this briefly in the last chapter but here we learn about the two types of expense in more detail.

CAPITAL EXPENDITURE includes:

- The purchase of NON-CURRENT ASSETS
- The improvement of the earning capability of non-current assets

Non-current assets are assets that are used in the business for more than one accounting period to provide benefits. These benefits are (we hope!) the profits earned from using the assets in the business. Plant and machinery, land and buildings, office equipment and motor vehicles are all examples of non-current assets that play their part in earning profits by being used within the business rather than being bought to make profit on their resale.

REVENUE EXPENDITURE includes:

- The purchase of materials for manufacture and goods for resale
- The maintenance of the existing earning capacity of non-current assets
- Expenditure incurred in conducting the business, including wages

In financial accounting terms, capital expenditure is shown as a non-current asset in the statement of financial position, while revenue expenditure is charged as a cost in the statement of profit or loss.

In management accounting terms, only revenue expenditure is considered.

It is, therefore, important to distinguish correctly between capital and revenue items, as this can hit profit quite hard given the large figures involved where non-current assets are concerned. It would mean that the statement of financial position does not show the correct cost of assets used by the business, and that the amounts included in the calculations of cost of items sold are inaccurate.

Depreciation

Over time even a non-current asset is 'used up' in the business so a charge in the statement of profit or loss is made each year of a certain amount of its cost. This is called DEPRECIATION and you will see a great deal more about it in the next stage of your studies. For now you need to know that depreciation charges on non-current assets are treated by management accounting as an expense in the period in question. Usually an equal amount is included in each year for each asset, which is called straight-line depreciation.

Some tricky items you may come across when deciding between capital and revenue categories involve changes to non-current assets and depreciation. Have a go at Task 1 and see if you can classify these items correctly.

Task 1

The table below lists some items that are either capital or revenue. Tick the correct box for each item.

	Capital	Revenue
Extension constructed onto a building		
Repairs to a machine		
Depreciation charge on a vehicle		
Installation of new machinery		
Redecorating offices		

CLASSIFICATION OF COSTS BY FUNCTION

Revenue expenditure can be further classified according to the function that causes the cost. The main functions within a manufacturing business give rise to the following cost classifications:

- **Production costs**. Materials and labour used to make the products, maintenance costs of the machinery and supervision of the workforce are examples of costs caused by the production function of a business.

- **Selling and distribution costs**. Advertising, delivery costs and sales staff salaries are caused by the selling and distribution function.

- **Administration costs**. The administration function gives rise to management, secretarial and accounting costs in co-ordinating the other functions of the business.

BPP
LEARNING MEDIA

- **Finance costs**. The finance function gives rise to all the expenses associated with raising money to finance the business, such as a loan or overdraft.

The distinction between these functions is not always clear, particularly when we are talking about administration costs, as there are no rules or regulations to follow, just commonsense. What is more, these are not the only possible functions within a business. Large companies often have a research and development function, or a training function; it depends on the type of business.

Task 2

Look at the list of costs below and decide whether each one would be classified as a production cost, a selling and distribution cost or an administration cost. Put a tick in the correct box.

Cost	Production cost	Selling and distribution cost	Administration cost
Factory rent			
Managing Director's salary			
Sales Director's salary			
Depreciation charge on office equipment			
Depreciation charge on plant and equipment			
Fuel for delivery vans			
Factory heating and lighting			

DIRECT AND INDIRECT COST ELEMENTS

A different way of classifying revenue expenses looks at the three major cost elements:

- Materials
- Labour
- Expenses, also known as OVERHEADS

Materials and labour are sub-divided into:

- DIRECT COSTS: costs which can be directly identified with a particular product or service provided

- INDIRECT COSTS: costs which cannot be directly identified with a product or service

Expenses/overheads are always treated as indirect costs for the purposes of this unit.

It is usually easy to identify the amount of a direct cost that is spent on one product or service, but it is more difficult to do so with indirect costs as they are not spent directly on one product or service: they are usually spent in relation to a number of products or services.

The resulting five cost classifications, and examples of these, are shown in the table below.

Direct materials	Materials incorporated into the finished product (eg wood used in the construction of a table).
Indirect materials	Materials used in the production process but not incorporated into the product (eg machine lubricants and spare parts). Insignificant costs that are attributable to each product are sometimes included in indirect materials for convenience (eg nails and glue for the table).
Direct labour	Wages paid to workers who make products in a manufacturing business (eg machine operators) or who perform the service in a service business (eg hairdressers in a hair salon).
Indirect labour	Wages and salaries of the other staff, such as supervisors, storekeepers and maintenance workers.
Indirect expenses	Expenses that are not spent on individual products or services (eg rent and rates, electricity and telephone).

In costing, the three types of indirect cost are often lumped together and called overheads.

OVERHEADS = Indirect materials + Indirect labour + Indirect expenses

We return to the topic of overheads in the next chapter when we cover cost behaviour.

Task 3

A building contractor employs a painter to paint the exterior and interior of the buildings they have built. Using the table below, tick the correct category of cost.

If the painter was doing maintenance work in a toy factory, which category of costs would this fall into?

	Direct cost	Indirect cost
Painter painting the building		
Painter doing maintenance work in the toy factory		

IDENTIFYING COST CENTRES

When we classify costs in this way we do so with the purpose of identifying them with the function or area or department of the business that they relate to, such as the production or administration function, the assembly or finishing area, or the human resources or marketing department. When we separate out the business into functions or areas or departments in this way, we can call each of them a COST CENTRE. All of the costs incurred by that cost centre are collected together and it is then possible to determine the total costs incurred by each cost centre for a period.

MATERIALS

In a manufacturing organisation materials are often the most significant cost involved in making products. The cost of the raw materials used in the production process is taken from the purchase invoice or from details of any cash purchases of raw materials that are made.

Analysing materials costs

When an invoice arrives from a supplier of raw materials it must be studied carefully as it needs to be analysed in a number of ways for management accounting purposes.

Step 1 Determine the quantity and cost of each type of material purchased as this is required for the records of the section of the business where materials are held – usually known as the stores department.

Step 2 Determine the cost of the materials being used by each of the business's cost centres.

HOW IT WORKS

You work in the accounts department of Wilmshurst Furniture Makers, a business that makes good quality wooden furniture – tables, chairs, desks, wardrobes and so on.

The manufacturing process involves three separate stages and therefore is split into three separate cost centres:

- Cutting – taking the wood and cutting it to the right size for each piece of furniture.

- Assembly – putting all of the pieces of wood together to form the finished item using glue, nails, screws etc.

- Polishing – preparing the furniture for eventual sale.

Given below is an invoice that has just been received from one of Wilmshurst's suppliers.

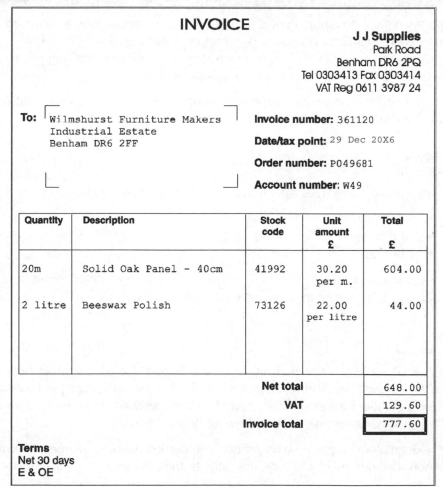

Quantity	Description	Stock code	Unit amount £	Total £
20m	Solid Oak Panel – 40cm	41992	30.20 per m.	604.00
2 litre	Beeswax Polish	73126	22.00 per litre	44.00
			Net total	648.00
			VAT	129.60
			Invoice total	777.60

INVOICE

J J Supplies
Park Road
Benham DR6 2PQ
Tel 0303413 Fax 0303414
VAT Reg 0611 3987 24

To: Wilmshurst Furniture Makers
Industrial Estate
Benham DR6 2FF

Invoice number: 361120

Date/tax point: 29 Dec 20X6

Order number: P049681

Account number: W49

Terms
Net 30 days
E & OE

Several pieces of information are required from this invoice:

- The stores department must update its records for the receipt of 20 metres of solid oak panel and two litres of beeswax polish. Often the stores records are kept only in terms of quantity, and the price is dealt with in the accounting department. However, if the stores records are also kept using price the unit prices of £30.20 per metre and £22.00 per litre respectively must be noted.

- The wood will be used by the cutting department, so the cost (**excluding** VAT of £604.00) must be charged to the cutting cost centre.

- The polish will be used by the polishing department and therefore its cost of £44.00 (again **excluding** VAT) must be charged to the polishing cost centre.

LABOUR

In the financial accounting records the cost of wages and salaries is shown in the wages expense ledger account. At its minimum it includes the GROSS PAY of the employees together with the employer's National Insurance Contributions. It may also include the employer's pension contributions, if any.

For management accounting purposes it is often necessary to analyse the gross pay of the employees in more detail.

Gross pay

The gross pay of employees can be made up of a number of different elements:

- Basic pay
- Overtime
- Bonus

We examine how each element is calculated in a later chapter but for the moment we will concentrate on what costs make up pay.

Basic pay

BASIC PAY is the amount that an employee is paid for their normal hours of work. Most employees will be employed on the basis that they are paid a certain rate for a certain number of hours a week. If they work for more hours than this in the week then overtime payments are made.

The hours that an employee works must be recorded in some manner. The most common methods are clock cards, time sheets and job cards.

A CLOCK CARD is a mechanical device, normally on the factory floor, which records the total time worked by an employee in a week by registering the time the employee arrives for work and leaves work. The clock card also records non-working hours such as lunch and tea breaks. In this way it can be determined precisely how many hours an employee has actually worked in the week.

A TIME SHEET is a method for employees to record for themselves the hours they have worked in a week and the precise work that has been done in those hours. Time sheets are often used in service industries and this is considered later in the chapter.

A JOB CARD is used in manufacturing businesses that produce large individual products such as aeroplanes or buildings. A job card relates to one of these large individual products and each employee that works on that job records the number of hours spent on it.

HOW IT WORKS

Jim Tyler works in the factory at Wilmshurst Furniture Makers. The terms of his employment are that his basic working week is 35 hours and his basic time-rate of pay is £8.60 per hour. For any hours over and above 35 a week he is paid overtime.

For Week 23 Jim's clock card shows that he has worked 35 hours in the week.

Therefore his gross pay for the week is made up solely of his basic pay and is calculated as:

35 hours @ £8.60 = £301.00

Analysis by cost centre

Many employees work for only one cost centre in which case the whole of their basic pay is collected as a cost for that cost centre.

However, some employees may have a variety of skills which mean that they work for a number of different cost centres in a week. The clock card shows which cost centres the employee has worked for and how many hours for each – the basic pay is then split between each of the cost centres.

HOW IT WORKS

Suppose that Jim's clock card shows that he worked in the cutting department for 24 hours during the week and in the assembly department for the remaining 11 hours.

His basic pay would be split between the two cost centres:

Cutting cost centre	24 hours @ £8.60	£206.40
Assembly cost centre	11 hours @ £8.60	£94.60

OVERTIME

OVERTIME is paid for any hours that employees work over and above the normal hours of work stated in their employment contract.

Overtime payments are normally expressed in terms of the time-rate for basic pay – the most common are:

- Time-and-a-half – this means that any overtime hours are paid at one-and-a-half-times the basic hourly time-rate

- Double time – overtime hours are paid at twice the basic hourly time-rate

HOW IT WORKS

In Week 39 Jim works for 29 hours in the cutting department and 12 hours in the assembly department – a total of 41 hours. He has therefore worked not only the 35-hour basic week but also six hours of overtime which were due to the amount of work in the cutting department.

We must calculate Jim's pay for the week:

	£
35 hours @ £8.60	301.00
6 hours @ £8.60 × 1.5	77.40
Total cost	378.40

The figure of £77.40 is the overtime payment to Jim – the full cost of working for the additional six hours at an overtime time-rate of £12.90 (1.5 × £8.60).

If all the overtime was caused by, say, the cutting department specifically asking Jim to work late it can be charged to that department:

	£
Cutting cost centre – labour cost 23 hours @ £8.60	197.80
Cutting cost centre – labour cost 6 hours @ £12.90	77.40
Assembly cost centre – labour cost 12 hours @ £8.60	103.20
	378.40

If the overtime was not caused specifically by one of the departments but was just required by pressure of work generally, the total cost of Jim's wages will be split between the cost centres in proportion to ('pro rata' with) the hours he worked there.

	£
Cutting cost centre – labour cost 29/41 hours × £378.40	267.65
Assembly cost centre – labour cost 12/41 hours × £378.40	110.75
	378.40

Alternatively the basic pay could be collected in the two cost centres as direct costs, and the overtime hours could be collected in an overall production cost centre as an indirect cost or overhead.

Task 4

Jan Simms works in the polishing department of Wilmshursts and her terms of employment are a 35-hour basic week with a basic rate of pay of £9.20 per hour and overtime paid at time-and-a-half. In week 32 she worked for 43 hours in total.

Calculate her basic labour cost and the overtime labour cost for the week.

	£
Basic labour cost	
Overtime labour cost	

BONUS PAYMENTS

In order to increase the productivity of employees, an employer will often set up a bonus scheme whereby the employee can earn additional pay over and above their basic pay if they work more efficiently. Bonus schemes may be on an individual basis or for a group of employees if they all work together on a particular task.

The bonus payment is usually charged to the relevant cost centre as an indirect cost/overhead although some organisations include it as part of the direct cost of labour for the cost centre.

EMPLOYER'S NATIONAL INSURANCE CONTRIBUTION

The wages cost of an employee is made up of their gross pay plus employer's NIC (and plus employer's pension contribution if any). Therefore the employer's NIC must also be charged to the relevant cost centre – sometimes this will be part of the direct labour cost but other organisations may include it as an expense/overhead.

HOW IT WORKS

As we have seen, Jim's gross pay for week 39 was £378.40. The employer's NIC is calculated as £36.02.

This figure of £36.02 will be charged to the relevant cost centres normally as an expense. In this case Jim worked for 29 hours in the cutting department and 12 hours in the assembly department therefore the employer's NIC will be split in this ratio:

Cutting cost centre – expense £36.02 × 29/41	£25.48
Assembly cost centre – expense £36.02 × 12/41	£10.54

EXPENSES

As well as using materials and labour, each cost centre may also incur some expenses (also known as overheads). Some of these expenses will be incurred specifically by the cost centre and others may be incurred jointly by a number of cost centres.

Specific expenses

Examples of expenses that might be directly incurred by a single cost centre may be:

- Cleaning costs of machinery
- Repair costs of machinery
- Lubricants for machinery

The details of these expenses will be taken from the invoice for the expense or other documentation that is associated with the expense.

HOW IT WORKS

The following two invoices have just been received by Wilmshurst Furniture Makers:

INVOICE	Invoice number 78473		
Ringrose Timber **Wootton Trading Estate** **Benham DR6 8AS**			
VAT registration:	78942 478 879		
Date/tax point:	28 December 20X6		
Order number:	763		
Customer:	Wilmshurst Furniture Makers		
Account number (customer code)	SL 891		
Description/product code	**Quantity**	**Per metre** £	**Total** £
Light oak 3 m lengths	2	10.65	63.90
Net total			63.90
VAT at 20%			12.78
Invoice total			76.68
Terms 30 days net			

INVOICE

D. P. Repairs Ltd
High Street
Benham DR6 4MS
Tel 0303610 Fax 0303611
VAT Reg 4321 1168 22

To: Wilmshurst Furniture Makers

Invoice number: 46123

Date/tax point: 28 Dec 20X6

Order number: -

Account number: SL 043

	Total
	£
Repair of X5461 Polishing machine	106.40
Net total	106.40
VAT	21.28
Invoice total	127.68

Terms
Net 30 days
E & OE

These expenses would be allocated to the cost centres as follows:

Cutting cost centre – expenses	£63.90
Polishing cost centre – expenses	£106.40

Note that, as with the materials cost, it is the net of VAT amount that is charged to the cost centre.

Joint expenses

Often the expenses of an organisation are incurred by a number of cost centres jointly. For example, when the rent is paid for the factory this will be an expense of all of the cost centres that are housed in the factory. In these cases the expense

must be split between the relevant cost centres and this is known as APPORTIONMENT OF COSTS.

The manner in which the expense is split between the cost centres that have incurred it will depend upon the policies of the organisation, using a fair basis to determine the split. For example with the rent expense this may be apportioned between the various factory cost centres according to the amount of floor space that each cost centre uses.

HOW IT WORKS

Wilmshurst Furniture Makers has recently incurred the following expenses:

Factory rent	£6,000
Factory power	£2,200

All three manufacturing departments are housed within the factory which has a total floor space of 12,000 sq metres. The rent is apportioned according to the floor space occupied:

Cutting	6,000 sq metres
Assembly	4,000 sq metres
Polishing	2,000 sq metres

It is estimated that 60% of the power is used by the cutting department, 15% by the assembly department and 25% by the polishing department.

The apportionment of the expenses would be:

Factory rent	Calculation	Apportioned amount
		£
Cutting	£6,000 × 6,000/12,000	3,000
Assembly	£6,000 × 4,000/12,000	2,000
Polishing	£6,000 × 2,000/12,000	1,000
Total		6,000

Factory power		
Cutting	£2,200 × 60%	1,320
Assembly	£2,200 × 15%	330
Polishing	£2,200 × 25%	550
Total		2,200

SERVICE ORGANISATIONS

We introduced service organisations in the previous chapter when we considered the different types of industry.

The largest type of cost for most service organisations is likely to be their labour cost. It was mentioned earlier in this chapter that the recording of employees' working hours in a service industry is often by use of time sheets. For example, in a firm of accountants each employee completes a weekly or monthly time sheet showing how many hours were worked not just in total, but on each particular client job in each department or cost centre. In a transport company, logs are kept for the hours driven by each driver.

As a service is being provided rather than a product made there are unlikely to be raw materials as such except for stationery, printer cartridges etc. These are often termed CONSUMABLES and are charged to the cost centres as they are used.

As with a manufacturing organisation, there is also a wide variety of expenses or overheads incurred which must be charged directly to each cost centre or apportioned between the cost centres.

Task 5

A delivery business has the following cost centres:

- Vehicle deliveries
- Motorbike deliveries
- Bookings
- Administration

The bookings and administration cost centres share the same building and use approximately half the space each. How would the following expenses be charged to the cost centres? Fill in the table below with your answer.

Rent and rates	£1,200.00
Repairs to motorbike	£240.00
Diesel for vans	£310.00

Cost centre	£
Vehicle deliveries	
Motorbike deliveries	
Bookings	
Administration	

CHAPTER OVERVIEW

- For management accounting purposes, costs are classified into the elements of materials, labour and expenses/overheads.

- Invoices for materials purchases must be analysed to determine the cost of the particular raw material (net of VAT) and which cost centre the material is to be used in.

- The total labour cost is gross pay plus the employer's NIC (and pension contribution if any) – gross pay can be made up of basic pay, overtime and a bonus.

- In order to determine the basic pay and any overtime, the actual hours that each employee works must be recorded – this is done on a clock card, a time sheet or a job card.

- Pay must be charged as a labour cost to the cost centre where the employee has worked during the period – if the employee has worked for more than one cost centre then each cost centre will be charged with the hours worked in the period.

- An employee is paid overtime for any additional hours worked over and above the basic hours in a week set out in the employment agreement, and this is also charged as a labour cost.

- If a bonus is earned, this is included as part of the gross pay – organisational policy will determine whether this is treated as a labour cost or an expense.

- Employer's NIC is part of the cost of labour and therefore must be charged to the relevant cost centre – again organisational policy will determine whether this is treated as part of the labour cost or as an expense.

- Expense invoices, net of VAT, should be analysed to determine which cost centre the expense relates to and charged to that cost centre.

- Some expenses relate to a number of different cost centres and need to be apportioned on an appropriate basis.

- Service organisations also classify their costs and charge them to the relevant cost centre – the main category of cost for most service industries is labour rather than materials or expenses.

- Service organisations usually do not have raw materials purchases but they do use materials in the business and these are known as consumables.

Keywords

Elements of cost – classifying costs into materials, labour and expenses

Capital expenditure – includes the purchase of non-current assets and the improvement of their earning capability

Non-current assets – are used in the business for more than one accounting period to provide benefits

Revenue expenditure – includes the purchase of materials for manufacture and goods for resale plus expenses incurred in the business

Depreciation charge – an expense in the statement of profit or loss to represent a proportion of the cost of a non-current asset

Overheads expenses incurred by the business that do not relate to materials or labour, treated as an indirect cost

Direct costs – can be directly identified with a product or service

Indirect costs – cannot be directly identified with a product or service

Cost centre – an area of the business for which costs are collected together for management accounting purposes

Gross pay – is made up of basic pay plus overtime and any bonus due

Basic pay – the amount paid to employees for their normal hours of work as agreed in the employment agreement

Clock card – a mechanical device on the factory floor that records the precise hours that the employee works for

Time sheet – a record of hours worked kept by the employee

Job card – a document on which is recorded all of the hours that each employee works on a particular job

Overtime – payment for the hours an employee works in a period over and above the agreed basic hours for the period

Apportionment of costs – the splitting of joint expenses amongst relevant cost centres on an appropriate basis

Consumables – materials that are used within a service industry although not used to make a product

TEST YOUR LEARNING

Test 1

Read the information given before attempting the question. Use the format given in the chapter for your answer.

Lara Binns works for Pole Potteries in both the throwing department and the baking department. Her employment agreement is that her basic week is 38 hours at a time-rate of £9.60 per hour. Any overtime is at double the time-rate.

During week 39 Lara worked for 26 hours in the throwing department and 15 hours in the baking department. All of the overtime hours were due to a backlog in the throwing department. The policy of Pole Potteries is to charge pay for all hours as the labour cost.

Show how the cost of employing Lara for week 39 would be analysed for management accounting purposes using the table below.

	£
Basic pay	
Overtime pay	
Total gross pay	
Cost centres	
Baking – labour	
Throwing – labour	
Total labour cost	

Test 2

Pole Potteries has recently received invoices for the following expenses:

Factory rent	£15,000
Warehouse rent	£5,000
Head office rent	£3,000
Cleaning of the throwing department	£200
Servicing of baking ovens	£600
Advertising	£400

The factory houses the following departments with the approximate percentage of floor space:

Throwing	15%
Baking	40%
Painting	15%
Maintenance	10%
Canteen	20%

The warehouse holds the stores and packaging departments and the stores use approximately 80% of this area.

The head office is small and consists of only selling and distribution (one cost centre) and administration, using equal amounts of space.

Calculate the expenses to be collected for each of the cost centres. Using the table below show your workings in your answer.

Cost centre	£
Throwing – expense – rent	
Throwing – expense – cleaning	
Throwing – Total	
Baking – expense – rent	
Baking – expense – servicing	
Baking – Total	
Painting – expense – rent	
Packaging – expense – rent	
Stores – expense – rent	
Maintenance – expense – rent	
Selling and distribution – expense – rent	
Selling and distribution – expense – advertising	
Selling and distribution – Total	
Canteen – expense – rent	
Administration – expense – rent	

Test 3

An accountancy firm has four cost centres: audit, tax, consultancy and administration. All are computerised and the latest purchase of printer cartridges for the central printers used by all departments totals £489.00 net of VAT. The estimated usage of printers is:

Audit	30%
Tax	40%
Consultancy	20%
Administration	10%

Calculate the allocation of the cost between the cost centres and show your workings.

Cost centre	£
Audit – consumables	
Tax – consumables	
Consultancy – consumables	
Administration – consumables	

Test 4

For a manufacturer of washing machines, classify the following costs by element (materials, labour or overheads) by putting a tick in the relevant column of the table below.

Cost	Materials	Labour	Expenses/overheads
Metal used for casing			
Business rates on warehouse			
Wages of operatives in assembly department			
Salary of factory supervisor			

Test 5

For a contract cleaning business, classify the following costs by nature (direct or indirect) by putting a tick in the relevant column of the table below.

Cost	Direct	Indirect
Detergent used for cleaning floors		
Depreciation of vacuum cleaner		
Wages of booking assistant		
Wages of cleaners		

Test 6

For a manufacturer of bricks, classify the following costs by function (production, administration, or selling and distribution) by putting a tick in the relevant column of the table below.

Cost	Production	Administration	Selling and distribution
Purchases of sand			
Fuel for salesperson's vehicle			
Printer paper for office			
Wages of factory workers			

chapter 3:
COST BEHAVIOUR

chapter coverage 📖

This chapter introduces you to expenses (or overheads) which are the indirect costs of the business. We also consider in more detail what is meant by cost centres, and consider profit centres and investment centres as well. The topics covered are:

- ✍ Fixed and variable overhead costs
- ✍ Cost, profit and investment centres
- ✍ Cost centres and service industries

FIXED AND VARIABLE OVERHEAD COSTS

In the last chapter we considered how costs are classified as materials, labour and expenses. We also saw how costs can be split between capital and revenue expenditure and by function, and how materials and labour costs can be split between direct or indirect costs.

We learnt that indirect materials and labour costs and expenses are also collectively called overheads. In this chapter we examine cost behaviour, and overhead cost behaviour in particular.

Costs can also be classified by their BEHAVIOUR, that is how the total cost is affected by a change in production level or activity level. Overheads are either variable, fixed or semi-variable depending on their behaviour. We will work through an example just now that gives you an idea of how the three types of cost behave. You will also find examples of overheads that fit into each of the three categories.

VARIABLE COSTS vary according to the level of production or activity. Each unit of output causes the same amount of cost to be incurred, so the total cost increases directly in proportion to the increase in output.

FIXED COSTS are the same over any level of activity, so they do not vary with changes in production or activity level.

SEMI-VARIABLE COSTS have an element of fixed cost and an element of variable cost.

HOW IT WORKS

Toys 4 U is a company that makes children's toys. One of its top selling lines is a "Chunker", a chunky plastic car that can be assembled by a child. The plastic components are bought-in at a cost of 90p per car. The company packages these in boxes which cost 20p each. The labour used for the packaging operation costs 20p per unit.

Each Chunker made has a variable cost of:

	£
Direct materials (90p + 20p)	1.10
Direct labour	0.20
Variable cost	1.30

If Toys 4 U made no Chunkers at all, there would be no cost at all. If it made ten Chunkers, it would cost £13. If it made 5,000 Chunkers, it would cost the company £6,500, and so on.

If we plot a graph of the total variable cost on the y-axis and the level of output on the x-axis, we would have an upward-sloping straight line which passes through the origin (0,0).

Graph of total variable cost

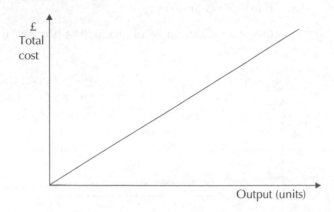

Direct materials and labour costs are generally all variable costs, although bulk discounts when purchasing materials may affect them. As a general rule, though, as the direct cost is spent directly on each unit of production, this will be the same amount for each unit, so a graph of **unit cost** against level of output would be a horizontal line; no matter how many are produced, the UNIT COST will be the same for each unit.

Graph of variable cost per unit

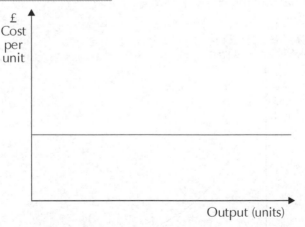

Overheads (indirect materials and labour costs, plus expenses) may also vary in line with output, for example, maintenance costs of a machine will increase if it is used more. Most overheads however, especially expenses, are FIXED COSTS

which are not affected by changes in production level. They remain the same in total whether no units are produced or many units. They are incurred in relation to a period of time rather than production level, and are sometimes referred to as period costs. Examples are the cost of lubricant for machinery for a year (indirect materials cost), the salary of a supervisor (indirect labour cost), the rent of a factory (expense) or straight-line depreciation of plant and machinery where the same amount is charged in each year (expense).

A graph of total fixed costs against output level produces a horizontal line.

Graph of total fixed costs

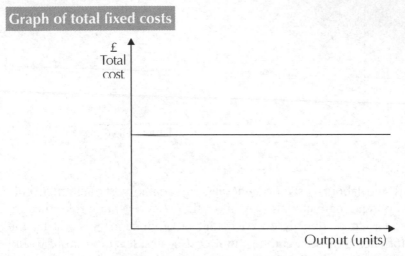

Because fixed costs remain the same at different output levels, if a fixed cost per unit is calculated, this will decrease as output increases as the same cost is spread over more units, so each unit attracts a smaller share. This gives management an incentive to increase production as it means that each unit is cheaper to produce. This is demonstrated in the graph below.

Graph of fixed cost per unit

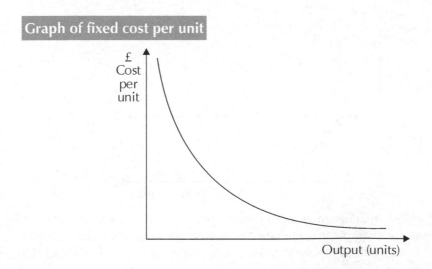

There are problems with calculating a fixed cost per unit however. One arises because many fixed costs are only fixed over a certain range of output. If the business decides to expand beyond a certain level, there will be a sudden jump in the cost to a new fixed amount. Such costs are STEP FIXED COSTS; the graph below demonstrates how they got their name . The rental of an extra factory unit, or the employment of another supervisor as the workforce increases beyond the limit which can be managed efficiently by one supervisor, would give rise to step fixed costs.

Graph of total step fixed costs

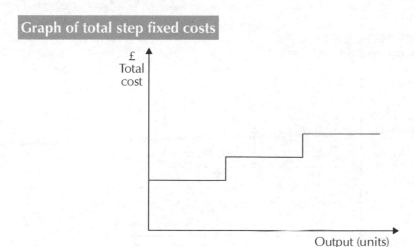

Task 1

Sleet Limited makes garden benches and incurs fixed costs of £20,000 per year. Calculate the fixed cost per garden bench at the following output levels, completing the entries in the table below.

Output level (units)	Fixed cost per bench £
1,000	
10,000	
20,000	
100,000	

A SEMI-VARIABLE COST is one which has both a fixed element and a variable element. One example of an overhead that is a semi-variable cost is electricity: the business faces a basic charge for the period plus a per unit consumption charge. Employees paid a basic wage plus commission are also a semi-variable cost.

The graph for a semi-variable cost in total is upward sloping, like the variable cost graph, but starts part of the way up the y-axis at the level of the fixed cost element.

Graph of total semi-variable costs

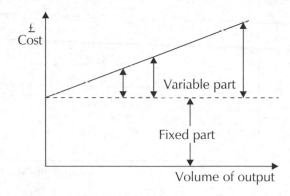

Cost behaviour and levels of activity

Knowledge of cost behaviour is essential when a business is planning its production levels and costs for the coming period. We'll work through an example which shows how the different types of cost are charged to production.

HOW IT WORKS

Cloudy Limited makes pencils and operates from a factory which costs £40,000 per annum to rent. The production line is largely mechanised and the depreciation of the machinery is £16,000 per annum. Both rent and depreciation are fixed over the range of output levels under consideration.

The variable costs per box of 100 pencils are:

- Raw materials and packaging – £1.20
- Labour – £1.60
- Expenses – £0.20

A supervisor is employed at £18,000 per annum to supervise the production line and inspect samples of the product. If production exceeds 500,000 boxes per annum another supervisor has to be employed on the same salary.

Cloudy Limited produced 400,000 boxes of pencils last year, but hopes to increase this to 600,000 next year as it has had enquiries from new customers. However, there is a threat of industrial action by one of its major raw material suppliers, and if it cannot source its raw materials from elsewhere, it will have to cut production by 50% to 200,000 boxes.

To analyse the effect of these possible activity levels on costs, a production schedule can be drawn up showing each of the three production levels. Variable costs can be found by multiplying the units of output by the variable cost per unit. Fixed costs remain the same at each output level. The amount included for the supervisor's salary will be one salary for 200,000 and 400,000 units, but two salaries if production is 600,000 units. This is a step fixed cost.

The estimated costs for the three possible production levels arc as follows.

Production costs

Production in units	200,000	400,000	600,000
	£	£	£
Costs			
Variable			
(units × (£1.20 + £1.60 + £0.20))	600,000	1,200,000	1,800,000
Fixed (40,000 + 16,000)	56,000	56,000	56,000
Step fixed	18,000	18,000	36,000
Total production cost	674,000	1,274,000	1,892,000
Cost per unit	£3.37	£3.18	£3.15

COST, PROFIT AND INVESTMENT CENTRES

A manufacturing business is likely to split naturally into a variety of different areas or departments. Typical examples may be:

- Cutting
- Assembling
- Finishing
- Packing
- Warehouse
- Stores
- Maintenance
- Administration
- Selling and distribution
- Finance

The precise split of a business will depend upon its nature and the nature of its activities and transactions. However the business is split up, managers need to know the costs and/or income of each department to be able to make decisions, plan operations and control the business.

Therefore each area or department which incurs costs only is known as a COST CENTRE. All of the costs incurred by that department are collected together and it is then possible to determine the costs incurred by each cost centre for a period.

Some of these cost centres are areas of the business that actually produce the products that the business sell – cutting, assembling, finishing etc. These are known as PRODUCTION COST CENTRES.

Other cost centres do not actually produce goods but are necessary to ensure that both production and sales take place – warehouse, stores, maintenance etc. These are known as SERVICE COST CENTRES as they provide a necessary service to the production cost centres.

Profit centres

We have seen that cost centres are areas of the business for which the costs incurred are all collected together. Some areas of a business incur costs but also earn income, and as income less costs equal profit, these are known as PROFIT CENTRES.

HOW IT WORKS

In a retail business, each individual shop produces income as well as incurring costs. Both costs and income for each shop are gathered together so each one is a PROFIT CENTRE. When the income and the costs are compared the final result will be the profit or loss made by the profit centre.

Task 2

In the table below, match the description to the type of cost centre.

Description	Production cost centre	Service cost centre	Profit centre
Cutting, assembling, packing			
Warehouse, stores, maintenance			
Retail shop			

Investment centres

There is a third classification for areas of the business for which costs (and income if relevant) are collected, and that is as an INVESTMENT CENTRE. This is when the business specifically calculates how much money or capital (measured as assets less liabilities) is invested in the respective area, and then usually 'charges' the area interest on the capital so it can get a true idea of how much real profit the area makes.

COST CENTRES AND SERVICE INDUSTRIES

So far in this chapter we have concerned ourselves mainly with manufacturing businesses. The unit also covers service industries and indeed you may work in the service sector, so the example below will be more familiar to you than a factory setting.

A service industry is a business that provides a service rather then producing a product, such as a firm of accountants, a painter and decorator or a transport organisation.

Service industries divide their businesses into cost centres, profit centres and investment centres in a similar manner to a manufacturing business.

HOW IT WORKS

A firm of accountants may have the following cost centres:

- Audit
- Tax
- Consultancy
- Administration
- Personnel
- Marketing

The audit, tax and consultancy departments may be designated as profit centres rather than cost centres so the income they earn is collected as well as the costs. A new branch of the firm may be designated as an investment centre as capital is needed to set it up.

CHAPTER OVERVIEW

- Revenue costs can be classified by several methods according to their behaviour: fixed; variable; step-fixed; semi-variable.

- Businesses tend to be split up into cost centres for management accounting purposes with the costs of each cost centre collected together.

- Profit centres are areas of the business which have income as well as costs, so not only are their costs collected together but also their income.

- Investment centres are areas of the business which have the amount of their assets and liabilities separately identified as well as their income and costs.

Keywords

Cost behaviour – the way a cost changes as production quantity or activity level changes

Variable costs – vary according to the level of production

Fixed costs– do not vary with changes in production level. They are incurred in relation to a period rather than a product

Semi-variable costs – costs which have both a fixed element and a variable element

Unit cost – the cost of each individual unit produced by the business or service provided

Step fixed costs – costs which are fixed over a certain range, but when output increases beyond a certain level, there will be a sudden jump in cost to a higher fixed amount

Production cost centres – cost centres that actually produce the products that are to be sold

Service cost centres – cost centres that provide support services to the production cost centres

Profit centre – an area of the business for which costs and income are collected together for management accounting purposes

Investment centre – an area of the business for which costs and income are collected plus the amount of capital (assets less liabilities) invested

TEST YOUR LEARNING

Test 1

Complete the following sketch graphs with the correct labels on each axis, and plot the cost.

(a) **Fixed costs**

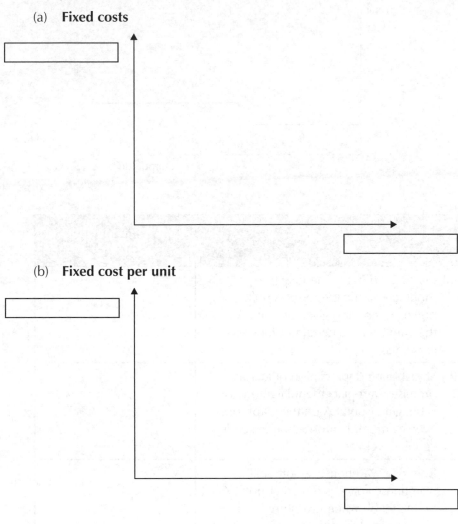

(b) **Fixed cost per unit**

Test 2

Look at the following sketch graph and then decide which of the suggested costs could be represented in that shape of graph. Complete each box in the table with 'yes' or 'no' as appropriate.

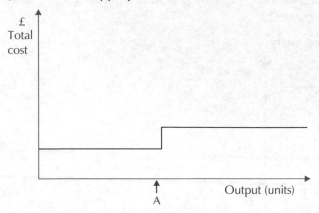

	Cost behaviour fits the graph shape?
(a) Plastic used in the manufacture of moulded plastic furniture. A bulk-buying discount is given at point A on the graph once a certain order size is exceeded.	
(b) Straight-line depreciation of factory premises; a replacement larger factory is bought at point A on the graph once average monthly production exceeds a certain level.	
(c) Rent of a warehouse. Additional warehouse space is rented at point A on the graph when inventory levels exceed a certain point.	
(d) Electricity costs which have a standing charge and a cost per unit of power used. At point A the level of production reaches the point where a nightshift is required, which uses electricity at a cheaper rate.	

Test 3

For a manufacturer of bags, classify the following costs by their behaviour (fixed, variable, or semi-variable) by putting a tick in the relevant column of the table below.

Cost	Fixed	Variable	Semi-variable
Entertainment budget for the year			
Telephone costs that include a fixed line rental charge plus call charges			
Leather used in the production process			
Labour costs paid as production overtime			

Test 4

Identify the following statements as either True or False by putting a tick in the relevant column of the table below.

	True	False
Total variable costs do not change directly with changes in activity but unit variable costs do		
Fixed costs per unit decrease with increasing levels of output		
The semi-variable cost curve shows a step change when an element of cost suddenly increases in amount		

chapter 4:
INVENTORY CLASSIFICATION AND VALUATION

---

chapter coverage 📖

This chapter looks at inventories. The topics covered are:

- ✍ Materials
- ✍ Types of inventory and inventory records
- ✍ Inventory valuation: FIFO, LIFO and AVCO methods
- ✍ Cost statement for manufactured goods (manufacturing account)

MATERIALS

We met materials in Chapter 2 when we considered how costs are classified. Now we look at the inventory of materials kept by the business, either for use in production or, ultimately, for resale.

TYPES OF INVENTORY AND INVENTORY RECORDS

INVENTORY is a collective term used to describe goods held by the business, and which (for this unit) can be included in one of the following categories:

- **Raw materials** and components for incorporation into products, and **consumables**

- **Finished goods** ready for sale and **goods purchased for resale**

- **Part-finished goods (work-in-progress or WIP)** which are that are only partially completed

Part-finished goods are an inevitable consequence of the way certain businesses are operated. If your business is making spoons, for example, there may be several stages in the production process:

- Stamping out the shape,
- Removing the rough edges, and
- Polishing.

An unfinished spoon at any point will be described as part-finished goods until it is fully polished. Some businesses will keep part-finished goods for a considerable time, such as makers of whisky which needs to be matured over a number of years. You will meet part-finished goods again in later units, but for the time being we are more concerned with the other categories of inventory.

Most businesses choose to keep inventories of materials and finished goods ready for when they are needed.

- Raw materials inventories are kept by a manufacturer so that materials are available for transfer to the production line when they are needed. Production would have to stop if there were no raw materials readily available, with several serious knock-on effects, such as labour being unable to work but still being paid, delay in producing the products and consequent dissatisfaction of customers. This would make the products more expensive for the business to manufacture. Goodwill might also be lost, meaning that customers would consider other suppliers in future.

- Consumable stores are needed so that there is no disruption of production or the administrative function of the business. For example, an inventory of printer cartridges is needed so that printing of plans and

diagrams (a production use of the printer), quotes for customers (sales), and letters and reports (administration) do not have to wait until more cartridges can be obtained.

- Finished goods are kept in inventory by a manufacturer so that demand from customers can be met and to avoid problems such as loss of goodwill.

- Goods for resale, which are the finished goods of manufacturers that have been bought for selling by retailers, are held so that changes in demand from day-to-day can be catered for. A shop would not be the same without an inventory of goods for the customer to look at and choose from!

Inventory records

Most businesses keep track of the quantities of raw materials that they have in inventory by maintaining an inventory record for each type of material held. This is updated each time material is received into, or issued from, stores, and a new balance of inventory held is calculated. This is known as a PERPETUAL INVENTORY system, and it can be manual or computerised.

There are two types of inventory record which may be kept, and sometimes they will both be used. These are inventory cards and stores ledger accounts.

Inventory cards

INVENTORY CARDS are manual records that are written up and kept in the stores department. An example is shown here.

INVENTORY CARD

Description: Blue plastic-coated fabric (1.8m wide)

Code No: B6309582

Inventory units: metres

Inventory No: 582

Maximum: 250

Minimum: 20

Reorder level: 40

Reorder quantity: 200

Receipts			Issues			Balance
Date	Reference	Quantity	Date	Reference	Quantity	Quantity
20X6			20X6			
1 May						40
11 May	GRN 0067	200				240
			12 May	MR 296	30	210
			14 May	MR 304	20	190
			15 May	MR 309	50	140
13 May	MRN 127	10				150

The information on the inventory card gives all the details the storekeeper needs to know:

- Description: of the inventory item for which this is a record.

- Inventory code: for unambiguous identification.

- Inventory units: the units in which the material is measured, eg metres, kilograms, boxes etc.

- Inventory number: the location of the items in the store.

- Inventory control information: maximum and minimum inventory levels, the level at which inventory needs reordering and the quantity to order. These details help the storekeeper to monitor the inventory levels and ensure they are maintained within required levels.

- Issues to production: date, quantity and a reference to the MATERIALS REQUISITION (MR), which is the document which the production department uses to request material from stores.

- Receipts: date, quantity and details of the GOODS RECEIVED NOTE (GRN) for goods delivered to the business. A GRN is raised in the goods inwards department to confirm the quantity and type of goods received from suppliers.

- Balance: the quantity of inventory on hand after each inventory movement.

Stores ledger accounts

The STORES LEDGER ACCOUNTS held by the accounts department are very similar to inventory cards. They carry all the information that an inventory card does, and they are updated from the same sources: GRNs and MRs. But there are two important differences:

(1) Cost details are recorded in the stores ledger account, so that the unit cost and total cost of each issue and receipt is shown. The balance of inventory after each inventory movement is also valued. The value is recorded as these accounts form part of the cost accounting system.

(2) The stores ledger accounts are written up and kept in the costing part of the accounts department, or in a stores office separate from the stores, by a clerk experienced in costing book-keeping.

Because inventory cards and stores ledger accounts are independent, they can be used as a control to check the accuracy of the records. The quantities of inventory recorded should be the same; if they are not, this has to be investigated and the appropriate adjustment made. An example of a stores ledger account is given later in this chapter where you can have a go at completing the details.

Materials requisitions

We saw earlier that a materials requisition (MR) is completed when materials are needed from stores by the production department. An official from production will sign the form to authorise it, and stores will issue the materials when the form is given to them. It is then used as a source document for:

- Updating the inventory card in stores
- Updating the stores ledger account in the accounts department
- Charging the job, overhead or department that is using the materials

The originating department fills in the materials requisition as shown below.

MATERIALS REQUISITION

Material required for: _Job 3965_   No: 296
(job)

Department: _Toy production_   Date: _12 May 20X6_

Quantity	Description	Code No	Price per unit	£
30	Blue plastic-coated fabric (1.8m wide)	B6309582		

Authorised by: .....J Daniels...................

The price details and value are filled in by the accounts department prior to updating the stores ledger accounts and charging the relevant job/overhead/department.

INVENTORY VALUATION: FIFO, LIFO AND AVCO METHODS

The stores ledger accounts record the value of materials purchased, and this information can be obtained from the supplier's invoice. When goods are issued from stores, a value needs to be recorded on the stores ledger accounts and on the costing details for the job or cost centre that is going to bear that cost. The question is: how do we value these issues if prices are changing regularly? Furthermore, how are the remaining inventories on hand valued?

Some items can be specifically priced from an invoice as they are individual items, but for most materials that are bought in quantity and added to an existing inventory this is not possible, so one of the following methods can be used to estimate the cost.

FIFO (First In, First Out)

This method assumes that the first items bought will be the first items issued. So as items are issued, the earliest invoice prices are used up first, working forwards through to the latest prices. The inventory on hand will always be valued at the later prices. This method is most appropriate in businesses where the oldest items are actually issued first, which is the case with perishable goods such as food, but actually this is a very popular method in many types of business.

LIFO (Last In, First Out)

This method assumes that the most recent purchases are issued first, as might be the case if new deliveries were physically piled on top of existing inventories, and goods issued were picked from the top of the pile. Issues are valued at the latest prices, working back through the records. This will tend to value remaining inventory on hand at earlier prices, which in times of general price inflation means a lower value of inventory than under FIFO.

AVCO (Average Cost)

With this method, a weighted average cost is calculated each time a new delivery is received. The weighting is provided by the number of units at each price brought into the calculation. The general formula is:

$$\text{Average price per unit} = \frac{\text{Total value of existing inventory} + \text{Total value of units added to inventory}}{\text{Units of existing inventory} + \text{Units added to inventory}}$$

AVCO would be most appropriate if the inventories were to be mixed when they are stored, for example chemicals stored in a vat, but again in practice this is a common method of valuation whatever the nature of the inventory.

HOW IT WORKS: FIFO, LIFO AND AVCO

Peregrine Pet Supplies sells doggy beds which it buys from a manufacturer. The following transactions were recorded in September 20X6:

Date	Transaction type	Quantity	Unit purchase price £
1 September	Opening balance	50	10
3 September	Purchase	100	12
6 September	Sell	110	
9 September	Purchase	100	13
15 September	Sell	80	
21 September	Purchase	100	14

What would be the:

(a) Cost of issues
(b) Value of closing inventory

in the month of September using FIFO, LIFO, and AVCO methods of valuation?

FIFO

Each time there is an issue of inventory, in this case in order to sell it, we must calculate the cost of those items based upon the first in, first out assumption.

6 September sale   110 units

These will be valued as 50 @ £10 and the remaining 60 @ £12 (purchased on 3 September).

    Total = £1,220

40 units are left in inventory at £12 each.

15 September sale   80 units

Of the 80 units sold, 40 will be valued @ £12 and the remaining 40 @ £13 (these were purchased on 9 September).

    Total = £1,000

60 units are left in inventory at £13 each. To these are added the 21 September purchase of 100 items at £14 each.

This can then all be recorded on the stores ledger account as follows:

		Quantity (units)	Cost per unit	Value £
1 Sept	Opening balance	50	£10	500
3 Sept	Purchase	100	£12	1,200
Balance		150		1,700
6 Sept	Sell	(110)	50 @ £10 + 60 @ £12	(1,220)
Balance		40		480
9 Sept	Purchase	100	£13	1,300
Balance		140		1,780
15 Sept	Sell	(80)	40 @ £12 + 40 @ £13	(1,000)
Balance		60		780
21 Sept	Purchase	100	£14	1,400
Balance		160		2,180

(a) Cost of issues. In this case the goods are issued to be sold:

= £1,220 + £1,000
= £2,220

(b) Value of closing inventory. This is the value of the balance on hand at the bottom of the calculation = £2,180. Note that this represents the latest items to be bought, 100 @ £14 + 60 @ £13.

You may also use the following format to complete a stores ledger account:

	Purchases			Sales			Balance	
Date	Quantity	Cost £	Total cost £	Quantity	Cost £	Total cost £	Quantity	Total cost £
Balance at 1 Sept							50	500
3 Sept	100	12.00	1,200				150	1,700
6 Sept				50	10.00	500	40	480
				60	12.00	720		
9 Sept	100	13.00	1,300				140	1,780
15 Sept				40	12.00	480	60	780
				40	13.00	520		
21 Sept	100	14.00	1,400				160	2,180

LIFO

This time the cost of the goods that are sold on each occasion will be determined under the last in, first out assumption.

6 September sale   110 units

These will be valued as 100 units @ £12 and the remaining 10 units @ £10.

Total = £1,300

40 units are left in inventory at £10 each.

15 September sale   80 units

Using the latest purchase price from the 9 September purchase these will all be valued at £13.

Total = £1,040

60 units are left in inventory, 20 from the 9 September purchase at £13 each and 40 from the opening balance at £10 each. To these are added the 21 September purchase of 100 items at £14 each.

Again this can be recorded in the stores ledger account as follows:

		Quantity (units)	Cost per unit	Value £
1 Sept	Opening balance	50	£10	500
3 Sept	Purchase	100	£12	1,200
Balance		150		1,700
6 Sept	Sell	(110)	100 @ £12 + 10 @ £10	(1,300)
Balance		40		400
9 Sept	Purchase	100	£13	1,300
Balance		140		1,700
15 Sept	Sell	(80)	80 @ £13	(1,040)
Balance		60		660
21 Sept	Purchase	100	£14	1,400
Balance		160		2,060

(a)   Cost of issues   = £1,300 + £1,040
                = £2,340

(b)   Value of closing inventory = £2,060

Note that this is **not** the same as valuing at the earliest prices (50 @ £10 + 100 @ £12 + 10 @ £13 = £1,830). This is because we have already used up some of those earlier prices in costing the earlier issues.

We could complete the entries in the LIFO stores ledger account as follows:

	Stores ledger account							
	Purchases			Sales			Balance	
Date	Quantity	Cost £	Total cost £	Quantity	Cost £	Total cost £	Quantity	Total cost £
Balance at 1 Sept							50	500
3 Sept	100	12.00	1,200				150	1,700
6 Sept				100	12.00	1,200	40	400
				10	10.00	100		
9 Sept	100	13.00	1,300				140	1,700
15 Sept				80	13.00	1,040	60	660
21 Sept	100	14.00	1,400				160	2,060

AVCO

Under the AVCO method a weighted average price must be calculated after each purchase. This average price is then used to value the next issue or sale. Here is the stores ledger account:

		Quantity (units)	Cost per unit	Value £
1 Sept	Opening balance	50	£10	500.00
3 Sept	Purchase	100	£12	1,200.00
Balance		150	£1,700/150 = £11.33	1,700.00
6 Sept	Sell	(110)	£11.33	(1,246.30)
Balance		40		453.70
9 Sept	Purchase	100	£13	1,300.00
Balance		140	£1,753.70/140 = £12.53	1,753.70
15 Sept	Sell	(80)	£12.53	(1,002.40)
Balance		60		751.30
21 Sept	Purchase	100	£14	1,400.00
Balance		160		2,151.30

(a) Cost of issues = £1,246.30 + £1,002.40
                              = £2,248.70

(b)   Value of closing inventory = £2,151.30

The alternative format for the AVCO stores ledger account is as follows (we have rounded to the nearest whole number for reasons of space):

Stores ledger account								
	Purchases			Sales			Balance	
Date	Quantity	Cost £	Total cost £	Quantity	Cost £	Total cost £	Quantity	Total cost £
Balance at 1 Sept							50	500
3 Sept	100	12.00	1,200				150	1,700
6 Sept				110	11.33	1,246	40	454
9 Sept	100	13.00	1,300				140	1,754
15 Sept				80	12.53	1,002	60	752
21 Sept	100	14.00	1,400				160	2,152

Task 1

Identify the correct inventory valuation method from the characteristic given by putting a tick in the relevant column of the table below.

Characteristic	FIFO	LIFO	AVCO
Issues are valued at the most recent purchase cost			
Inventory is valued at the most recent purchase cost			
Issues are valued at the average of the cost of purchases			

COST STATEMENT FOR MANUFACTURED GOODS

Many manufacturing businesses are quite complex and have a variety of inventory lines, including materials, part-finished goods and finished goods for resale. For both financial and management accounting purposes they need to identify a figure for the cost of goods they have actually sold rather than retained as inventory in a period, and to do this they prepare a COST STATEMENT FOR MANUFACTURED GOODS or MANUFACTURING ACCOUNT. This statement is prepared on the basis that only the costs of manufacturing the actual goods sold are included. To do this we must:

- add in the cost of inventory held at the beginning of the period (of raw materials, part-finished goods and finished goods)

- add in the cost of direct raw materials purchased, direct labour and manufacturing overheads incurred in the period

- deduct the cost of inventory (of all types) held at the end of the period, since these are carried forward and used up in the next period.

HOW IT WORKS

Lama Ltd manufactures a range of products from a large number of raw materials. It has produced the following cost statement for manufactured goods.

Lama Ltd: Cost statement for manufactured goods for the year ended 31 March 20X9

	£
Opening inventory of raw materials	6,000
Add: purchases of raw materials	70,000
Less: closing inventory of raw materials	(8,000)
DIRECT MATERIALS USED	68,000
Direct labour	37,900
DIRECT COST	105,900
Manufacturing overheads (eg supervisor salary, factory rent, machine depreciation, factory light and heat):	35,000
MANUFACTURING COST	140,900
Add: opening inventory of part-finished goods	4,000
Less: closing inventory of part-finished goods	(4,900)
FACTORY COST OF GOODS MANUFACTURED	140,000
Add: Opening inventory of finished goods	56,000
Less: Closing inventory of finished goods	(47,000)
COST OF GOODS SOLD	149,000

Let's look at some of the terms introduced here (you need to learn what each of the capitalised elements of this cost statement means for your assessment).

DIRECT MATERIALS USED is the cost of materials purchased in the period, plus the cost of opening inventory less the cost of closing inventory.

DIRECT COST (sometimes known as prime cost) is the total cost of direct material and direct labour.

MANUFACTURING COST is the direct cost plus manufacturing overheads (expenses relating to manufacturing).

FACTORY COST OF GOODS MANUFACTURED includes the net change in the inventory of part-finished goods in the period. Sometimes this is referred to just as 'Cost of goods manufactured'.

COST OF GOODS SOLD is therefore opening inventory (of all items) plus purchases, direct labour and manufacturing overheads less closing inventory of all items.

CALCULATING PRODUCT COST

Having prepared the information that goes into the cost statement, we need to understand what it actually tells us.

A cost statement that covers a whole organisation, like Lama Ltd's, takes into account all product lines and all raw materials, direct labour and overheads so it tells us how much it cost the organisation to produce all the goods which it actually sold in the period in question. This means it can calculate its GROSS PROFIT overall, a financial accounting figure that appears in the published statement of profit or loss:

	£
Revenue	X
Cost of goods sold	(X)
Gross profit	X

If the organisation only has one product, or if the cost statement only relates to one product, we can use it to calculate a PRODUCT COST per unit of output. This is also sometimes known as a unit cost.

HOW IT WORKS

Pringle Ltd makes and sells only one product in a simple process that means there are no part-finished goods. It has prepared the following cost statement, for a period when it made 100,000 items and sold 120,000 items:

	£
Opening inventory of raw materials	5,000
Add: purchases of raw materials	49,000
Less: closing inventory of raw materials	(9,000)
DIRECT MATERIALS USED	45,000
Direct labour	105,000
DIRECT COST	150,000
Manufacturing overheads	55,000
MANUFACTURING COST (100,000 items)	205,000
Add: Opening inventory of finished goods (30,000 items)	56,000
Less: Closing inventory of finished goods (10,000 items)	(21,000)
COST OF GOODS SOLD (120,000)	240,000

There are three useful figures that we can calculate from this information:

- The DIRECT COST (direct materials plus direct labour) of each of the 100,000 items manufactured in the period is £150,000/100,000 = £1.50 each.

- If manufacturing overheads are added in, the PRODUCT COST of each of the 100,000 items manufactured is £205,000/100,000 = £2.05 each.

- The COST OF GOODS SOLD in the period is £240,000/120,000 = £2.00 each.

You may be wondering why the product cost and the cost of goods sold are different amounts. This arises because the goods sold include both opening inventory (which we can see cost £56,000/30,000 = £1.87 each) as well as items produced in the period at £2.05 each. The effect of this is to bring the average cost per unit of goods sold down to only £2.00.

CHAPTER OVERVIEW

- Materials can be made up of raw materials for use in production, part-finished goods and finished goods.

- The quantity of each line of inventory will often be recorded on an inventory card – a stores ledger account is similar but this also includes the value of the inventory held.

- When materials are required from stores by a production or other department the user department will issue a materials requisition detailing the goods required.

- The valuation of inventory normally requires an assumption to be made regarding the valuation method – this will be FIFO, LIFO or AVCO.

- A cost statement for manufactured goods identifies the cost of goods sold in a period.

- The cost statement can also be used to calculate product cost per unit manufactured.

Keywords

Inventory – goods held by the business made up of raw materials including consumables, part-finished goods and finished goods

Perpetual inventory – a continuously updated inventory record system showing receipts, issues and the resulting balances of individual inventory lines: **inventory cards** are usually maintained in the stores department and are in terms of quantity; **stores ledger accounts** are kept in the accounts department and show values as well

Goods received note (GRN) – a document raised in the goods inwards department to confirm the quantity and type of goods received by them for the business's own records

Materials requisition – a request for materials by the production department sent to stores

FIFO (first in, first out) – assumes that the earliest purchases are used first. Inventory on hand is valued at the latest prices, issues at the earlier prices at the time of issue

LIFO (last in, first out) – assumes that the latest purchases are used first. Inventory on hand is valued at earlier prices and issues are valued at the latest prices at the time of the issue

AVCO (average cost) – a weighted average cost is calculated each time a delivery is received. Subsequent issues and inventory on hand are valued at the most up-to-date weighted average cost

Cost statement for manufactured goods or **manufacturing account** – a statement that analyses costs to show the cost of goods sold by a business

Direct materials used – the cost of materials purchased in the period, plus the cost of opening inventory less the cost of closing inventory of materials

Direct cost – the total cost of direct material and direct labour used

Manufacturing cost – direct cost plus manufacturing overheads

Factory cost of goods manufactured – manufacturing cost plus net inventory of part-finished goods

Cost of goods sold – represents opening inventory (of all items) plus purchases, direct labour and manufacturing overheads less closing inventory of all items

Product cost – the cost of each item manufactured if the full costs of direct materials, direct labour and manufacturing overheads are included

TEST YOUR LEARNING

Test 1

Classify the following items as raw materials, part-finished goods or finished goods. (Tick the appropriate box.)

	Raw materials	Part-finished goods	Finished goods
Bricks at a brick-making factory			
Bricks in stores at a building company			
The ingredients for making bricks held in stores			
A brick that has been moulded but not fired in the kiln			

Test 2

Using the:

    (a)   FIFO

    (b)   LIFO

    (c)   AVCO

methods, calculate the cost of materials issues and the value of closing inventory using the information below, and enter these into the stores ledger account. Show your workings underneath the account.

3 Jan	Balance	100 kg	Valued @ £8.80 per kg
16 Jan	Received	400 kg	£9 per kg
27 Jan	Issued	250 kg	
5 Feb	Issued	180 kg	
9 Feb	Received	400 kg	£9.30 per kg
17 Feb	Issued	420 kg	
25 Feb	Received	500 kg	£9.35 per kg

FIFO

Stores Ledger Account									
	Purchases			Sales				Balance	
Date	Quantity (kg)	Cost £	Total cost £	Quantity (kg)	Cost £	Total cost £		Quantity (kg)	Total cost £

LIFO

Stores Ledger Account

Date	Purchases			Sales			Balance	
	Quantity (kg)	Cost £	Total cost £	Quantity (kg)	Cost £	Total cost £	Quantity (kg)	Total cost £

AVCO

Stores Ledger Account									
	Purchases			Sales			Balance		
Date	Quantity (kg)	Cost £	Total cost £	Quantity (kg)	Cost £	Total cost £	Quantity (kg)	Total cost £	

Test 3

Identify whether the following statements are True or False by putting a tick in the relevant column of the table below.

Characteristic	True	False
FIFO costs issues of inventory at the oldest purchase price		
AVCO costs issues of inventory at the most recent purchase price		
LIFO costs issues of inventory at the most recent purchase price		
FIFO values closing inventory at the oldest purchase price		
LIFO values closing inventory at the oldest purchase price		
AVCO values closing inventory at an average purchase price		

Test 4

A business has the following movements in a certain type of inventory into and out of its stores for the month of October:

Date	Receipts		Issues
	Units	Cost	Units
3 Oct	200	£360	
7 Oct	160	£360	
11 Oct			90
19 Oct	100	£240	
24 Oct	70	£160	

Complete the table below for the cost of the issue on 11 October and the value of closing inventory on 31 October.

Method	Cost of issue on 11 Oct	Closing inventory at 31 Oct
FIFO		
LIFO		
AVCO		

chapter 5:
CLASSIFYING LABOUR COSTS

chapter coverage 📖

This chapter looks at one of the major costs that a business incurs which is labour. This unit asks you to explain methods for calculating payments for labour so we cover that here. The topics covered are:

✎ Labour costs

✎ Remuneration methods

✎ Recording labour costs

LABOUR COSTS

For management accounting purposes it is often necessary to analyse the gross pay of employees in detail. In Chapter 2 we introduced the terms you need to know and showed you how basic pay, overtime, national insurance and bonuses are calculated. Later in this chapter these calculations are used when looking at different remuneration methods.

We mainly talk about the gross pay of the employee, but don't forget that there are other costs which can be considered to be labour costs, such as employer's national insurance, employer's pension contributions, training costs and benefits such as company cars. All employees give rise to labour costs: office workers in administration departments, canteen staff, maintenance staff and supervisory staff are examples of **indirect labour** which we looked at in Chapter 2. **Direct labour** costs arise from the employees who work directly on the goods produced by a manufacturing business, or employees who provide the service in a service business.

REMUNERATION METHODS

A number of different remuneration methods exist, the bases of which are given below. These are the simplest situations; combinations of these methods and variations on the basic ideas can lead to more complicated methods of remuneration.

Time-rate

A TIME-RATE means that a basic amount is paid per hour worked.

> Wages = hours worked × basic rate of pay per hour

This method of remuneration is fairly simple to understand, and does not lead to complicated negotiations when rates of pay are being revised. It is appropriate if the quality of the output is more important than the quantity but it gives no incentive to improve performance. This is because workers will be paid so much per hour no matter how many items they produce. A plus point for a time-rate system is that workers will not feel that they have to rush, so quality can take priority.

If the hours worked exceed a pre-set maximum, OVERTIME is paid at a higher overtime time-rate. In the assessment you may well be asked to calculate the gross pay for labour, separating out the cost of hours at the basic time-rate from the cost of hours at the overtime time-rate.

HOW IT WORKS

Finch Limited has an overtime time-rate of time-and-a-third for all complete hours worked over 35 hours per week. Peter is paid a basic wage of £6 per hour. During the week ending 24 March he worked a total of 39 hours. Work out Peter's gross pay for the week.

	£
Basic hours at time-rate (35 × £6)	210
Overtime hours at overtime time-rate (4 × £6 × $1^1/_3$)	32
Gross pay for the week	242

Some businesses treat basic pay for all hours worked as a direct cost, but the amount paid extra for overtime (called the 'overtime premium') as an indirect cost for costing purposes. This way, all units produced are costed at the basic labour cost, irrespective of whether they were produced during normal working hours or at the weekend, for example, when overtime was being paid.

HOW IT WORKS

The total overtime pay in the case of Finch Ltd is £32. This comprises two elements:

(a) The basic element is the basic pay time-rate × additional hours worked, in this case 4 hours × £6 = £24.

(b) The OVERTIME PREMIUM is the extra paid on top of the basic rate for the additional hours worked. In this case the hourly premium is £6 × 1/3 = £2. The total overtime premium is therefore 4 hours × £2 = £8. It is this amount that some businesses may treat as an indirect cost, with the remainder of gross pay – £234 – treated as direct labour cost.

Note however that if the overtime is worked at the request of a customer so that the order can be completed within a certain time, the overtime premium is a direct cost of that particular order.

Task 1

Pauline is paid £10 per hour for a 37-hour week as an assembly worker. She is paid overtime at time-and-a-half. Overtime premium is treated as an indirect cost. Calculate the direct and indirect labour cost incurred if Pauline works for 41 hours in a particular week. Fill in the table below.

	Direct cost £	Indirect cost £
Basic pay		
Overtime: basic		
Overtime: premium		
Gross pay		

Piecework

With PIECEWORK, an amount is paid for each unit or task successfully completed, acting as an INCENTIVE to produce more. This method of remuneration can only be used in certain situations, ie when there are specific, measurable tasks to be done which are not affected by other employees' performances.

DIFFERENTIAL PIECEWORK offers higher rates as production increases. For example, 5p per unit is paid for production of up to 2,000 units per week, rising to 7p per unit for 2,001 to 3,000 units, and so on.

Task 2

Simon sews pockets in a tailoring factory. He is paid 10p for every pocket sewn up to a total of 4,000 in one week. Thereafter, he receives an extra 2p per additional pocket up to 500 additional pockets; his rate further increases by 2p for each 500 further pockets. One week he sews 4,730 pockets. What will his gross pay be in that week? Put your answer in the table below.

Number of pockets	Gross pay £
4,000	
500	
230	
Total	

Bonus systems

A BONUS SYSTEM involves paying a bonus if output is better than expected. This will be in addition to the normal time-rate. The trigger for the payment of a bonus depends on the type of system that operates.

- A time-saved bonus is paid if the employee performs a task in a shorter time than the standard time allowed.

- A discretionary bonus is paid if the employer judges that the employee deserves one.

- A group bonus scheme pays a bonus to all workers who contributed to a successful job.

- A profit-sharing scheme pays a proportion of the business's profits to employees, the size of the proportion paid often reflecting the level of responsibility.

This system can operate at all levels in any business, and can give an incentive for workers to produce more with the security of their basic time-rate. As with piecework, though, a bonus system can be complex to calculate and will need quality control checks.

Salary

Employees on a monthly SALARY are paid one-twelfth of their agreed annual salary each month. Overtime, bonuses and commissions on sales, for example, can be paid on top of this. Salaries tend to relate to indirect labour, such as office staff and factory supervisors. In the service sector, though, many salaried staff are a direct cost of providing the service, such as solicitors and accountants.

HOW IT WORKS

Osprey Fish Co buys fresh fish, prepares the fish for sale in supermarkets and distributes its products throughout the UK using its own fleet of delivery vehicles.

(a) Steven works part-time filleting the fish and is paid on the following basis:

	£ per fish
Trout	0.20
Haddock	0.24
Salmon	0.30

In the week ending 24 November, Steven filleted 290 trout, 480 haddock and 395 salmon.

Steven's gross pay for the week ending 24 November is calculated as follows:

Gross pay = (290 × £0.20) + (480 × £0.24) + (395 × £0.30)
            = £ 291.70

(b)   Shirley is a mechanic for the delivery vehicles, who earns £9 per hour for a 40-hour week. She is paid overtime at time-and-a-quarter, and earns a bonus of £5 for each job on which she makes a time saving of 5% or more on the standard time. In the week ending 24 November she works a total of 43 hours and qualifies for bonus payments in respect of five jobs performed.

Shirley's gross pay for the week ending 24 November includes basic hours at the time-rate plus overtime at the overtime time-rate plus time-saved bonus.

	£
Pay (40 hours × £9)	360.00
Overtime : basic (3 hours × £9)*	27.00
Overtime: premium (3 hours × £9 × 0.25)*	6.75
Bonus (5 jobs × £5)	25.00
Gross pay	418.75

*The overtime could just be calculated at the overtime time-rate: 3 hours x £9 x 1.25 = £33.75

(c)   Patrick works in the sales office. His contract of employment specifies a 1,820 hour year and an annual salary of £15,000 per year. Any hours worked in excess of the contractual weekly amount are paid at Patrick's basic time-rate. In the month of November he works a total of 15 hours overtime.

Patrick's gross pay for November basic pay plus overtime:

	£
Basic salary (£15,000 / 12)	1,250.00
Overtime (£15,000/1,820 × 15)	123.63
Gross pay	1,373.63

In this case, we had to work out a basic hourly time-rate by dividing the annual salary by the total number of contractual hours in a year under the contract. This was then used to work out how much Patrick could be paid for overtime.

Task 3

For each of the statements in the table below, put a tick against the correct rate in the appropriate box.

	Time-rate	Piecework rate
Easy to calculate an employee's pay		
Can be used for all direct labour employees		
More efficient workers are paid more than less efficient workers		
The quality of the goods produced is affected by workers being tempted to rush a job so that they earn more		
The employees' basic pay fluctuates if output fluctuates		
More supervisors may be needed for this system		
Production problems can lead to a cut in pay		
Systems need to be set up to check the amount of work produced by each employee		

RECORDING LABOUR COSTS

Information on labour hours worked and rates of pay is needed by two departments:

- The payroll department needs to know so that the amount that each employee has earned can be worked out.

- The costing department needs to know so that the labour cost of each task or unit of product can be calculated.

The human resources (HR) department maintains records of each employee's contract of employment and basic rate of pay. It issues the payroll department with a list of employees and rates of pay, usually via a database containing basic pay and overtime time-rates, piecework rates etc.

The time worked by each employee is recorded on various types of document, depending upon the nature of their employment.

Attendance time records

Sometimes, all that needs to be recorded is the attendance of the employee at the place of work. This can be achieved by using one of the following:

- **Attendance record**. Essentially a calendar for an individual, a tick in the box records the presence of the employee at work on that day. If absent, the reason (sickness, holiday etc) can be indicated.

- **Signing-in book**. This book has a page for each employee, and is signed by the employee when entering or leaving the building, or when a break is taken. This allows a more accurate calculation of time worked.

- **Clock cards**. Each employee has a card which is entered in a time recording clock as work is commenced and finished. The time is recorded on the CLOCK CARD which is then used for pay calculations. Computerised systems perform the same function by means of a plastic swipe card. The time is recorded by the computer rather than on the card.

Job costing

Many businesses perform work on particular jobs or tasks, often for particular clients, such as a construction company building an office block, a manufacturer of complex or unique items such as train rolling stock, or an accountancy firm conducting an audit. In such cases it is important to collect together all the costs, including labour costs, that relate to each particular job, not least because this may affect how much the client is charged. This is called JOB COSTING.

Where an employee works on more than one job in a day or a week, more detailed analysis of time worked needs to be recorded so that the jobs can be costed. Note that attendance time records will also, generally, be kept for payroll purposes.

- TIMESHEETS are used to record the time spent by an employee on each job that they have worked on. Timesheets are passed to the costing department daily (**daily timesheets**), or weekly if there are few job changes in a week (**weekly timesheets**). Timesheets are often used in the service sector, for example accountants will fill in a weekly timesheet showing the number of hours and the clients for whom they have performed accounting services during that week.

- JOB CARDS are prepared for each job or an operation on a larger job. The job card will describe the task to be performed. The employee will fill in the start and finish times of the job, and time out for any breaks. The card will be completed in the accounting department where the cost of that job can be calculated.

JOB CARD

Job No   824

Date

Time allowed   2 hours   **Start time**

                                Finish time

Job description	Hours	Rate	Cost £
Apply dark oak varnish to the exterior surfaces			

Employee number   ....

Employee signature   ....

Supervisor's signature ....

- ROUTE CARDS are similar to job cards, but they detail all the operations to be carried out on a job, rather than just one, and will follow the job through to completion. As each operation is completed, the relevant employee will enter the time spent on it. The full cost of the job will gradually build up on the route card.

Usually the data required is captured electronically.

Job costing systems will be considered in more detail in units at level 3.

Piecework

A **piecework ticket** (or **operation card**) is used to record the number of units produced in a piecework system. Piecework tickets are very similar to job cards, and are used for each operation performed on a batch of units. The worker records the number of units completed, the number of rejects, and the number of good units; they are only paid for good production. A supervisor and an inspector are required to sign the ticket to validate the quantities.

CHAPTER OVERVIEW

- Remuneration methods generally fall into one of the following categories:

    - Time-rate and overtime time-rate
    - Piecework
    - Bonus system
    - Salary

- Employees record their attendance times on attendance records, signing-in books or clock cards.

- Job costing requires more detailed records of time spent on each job, and this is recorded on a timesheet, a job card or a route card.

- Piecework is recorded on a piecework ticket (or operation card).

Keywords

Time-rate – a basic amount per hour is paid

Overtime time-rate – a higher rate of pay if hours worked in a week exceed a pre-set limit

Overtime premium – the additional cost of overtime hours above the basic time-rate for those hours

Piecework – an amount is paid for each unit or task successfully completed

Incentive – in piecework systems, the incentive of being paid to complete each extra unit or task encourages the worker to increase their output

Differential piecework – the piecework rate increases for additional units over and above a pre-set quantity

Bonus system – the payment of an amount in addition to the time-rate or salary if a target is exceeded

Salary – the payment of a set amount at agreed intervals, usually weekly or monthly

Clock card – a card for each employee that records the start and finish times of periods of work

Job costing – collecting together all the costs related to a particular large job or task

Timesheet – a form completed by an employee detailing the time spent on each client's work each day, or week

Job card – records the time spent by the employee on a job

Route card – details the task to be performed on a particular job, and follows the job round; each employee records the time spent on their operation on the job

TEST YOUR LEARNING

Test 1

Mary Dunnock works in Pole Potteries making wooden lids. The piecework rate for milling each lid is 14p. Calculate Mary Dunnock's gross pay for the week ended 7 July 20X6 by completing her operation card.

OPERATION CARD

Operator	Mary Dunnock	Works order No	1492
Clock No	16	Part No	233
Week ending	7.7.X6	Description	Wooden lids

Operation Sanding top and bottom surface using grade 2 sandpaper

Quantity produced	Quantity rejected	Good production	Rate £	£
Monday 350	12			
Tuesday 428	21			
Wednesday 483	2			
Thursday 376	14			
Friday 295	18			

Employee number   *352*   Date   7.7.X6

Employee signature   *MD*

Supervisor's signature   *S Ditford*

Test 2

Cockerel Breakfast Cereals Limited pays a time-rate of £7 per hour for a 35-hour week. Overtime is paid at time-and-a-half for time worked in excess of seven hours on weekdays, and double time for any work done at the weekend.

Calculate the gross pay of the employees whose clock card information is summarised below and enter the details in the table below.

Hours worked				
	J Sparrow	K Finch	M Swallow	B Cuckoo
Monday	7	7	7.25	7
Tuesday	7	8	7	7
Wednesday	7.5	7	7.5	7
Thursday	8	8	7.5	7.5
Friday	7	7.5	7.5	7
Saturday	3		2	2

	J Sparrow	K Finch	M Swallow	B Cuckoo
Total hours				
Basic pay	£	£	£	£
Time-and-a-half	£	£	£	£
Double time	£	£	£	£
Total gross pay	£	£	£	£

Test 3

Identify the labour payment method by putting a tick in the relevant column of the table below.

Payment method	Time-rate	Time-rate plus bonus	Piecework	Differential piecework
Employees are paid for the hours worked and receive an incentive if a target is reached				
Employees are paid for output achieved and receive an incentive as production increases				
Employees are paid only for output achieved				
Employees are only paid for the hours worked				

chapter 6:
CODING COSTS

---

chapter coverage 📖

We have seen how the elements of cost should be collected by each cost centre. In this chapter we see how this is done by coding the invoices and payroll information in order to achieve the accurate collection of these costs. The topics covered are:

✍ Methods of coding

✍ Coding the elements of cost. Coding materials costs, labour costs and expenses

✍ Updating cost, profit and investment centre balances

METHODS OF CODING

We have already seen how each cost incurred by the business must be analysed and then charged to the correct cost centre as materials, labour or an expense. In order for this to happen the expenditure must be coded to show what type of cost it is and which cost centre it is to be charged to.

Each business will have its own coding structure. Here we consider various methods of coding: alphabetic coding systems, numeric coding systems and alpha-numeric coding systems.

In general terms, most businesses probably arrange their ledger accounts into groups representing the different accounting aspects of the business. For example the groups of accounts that may be required might be:

- Income accounts
- Expenses accounts
- Asset accounts
- Liability accounts
- Capital accounts

Within each of the groups the ledger accounts may again be split into sub-groups, for example within asset accounts there may be non-current asset accounts and current asset accounts. If there are investment centres in the business – for example Site A and Site B - then these asset accounts may be further split into 'non-current assets account Site A' and 'non-current assets account Site B' etc.

There are many coding systems in practice and each business will choose one that suits its transactions and operations. Probably the two most common methods are NUMERIC CODING and ALPHA-NUMERIC CODING. Purely alphabetic systems may also be used, but these tend to be rather confusing to use.

A numeric coding system is where the code is entirely numerical. For example the general ledger codes might be set up as follows:

Income accounts	0001 – 0199
Expenses accounts	0200 – 0499
Asset accounts	0500 – 0699
Liability accounts	0700 – 0899
Capital accounts	0900 – 1000

There are potentially 1,000 ledger accounts here. They do not all have to be used but the coding system must be flexible enough to allow for new accounts to be opened up.

An alpha-numeric coding system uses a mixture of letters and numbers to code the ledger accounts. For example the general ledger account codes might alternatively be set up as:

Income accounts	A001 – 200
Expenses accounts	B001 – 200
Asset accounts	C001 – 200
Liability accounts	D001 – 200
Capital accounts	E001 – 200

An alphabetic coding system uses just letters to code the ledger accounts. For example the general ledger account codes might alternatively be set up as:

Income accounts	AAA – DZZ
Expenses accounts	EAA – JZZ
Asset accounts	KAA – PZZ
Liability accounts	QAA – VZZ
Capital accounts	WAA – ZZZ

Once the coding system has been set up, when entries are made in, for instance, the cash book and are referenced to the general ledger then the reference would include the account code for that ledger account.

A coding system does not have to be structured entirely on any one of the above systems. It can mix the various features according to the items which need to be coded.

CODING THE ELEMENTS OF COST

Materials

We have already seen that the net amount of each purchase invoice that arrives must be analysed to determine the type of cost and the cost centre to which it should be charged. Each element of the invoice must then be coded to ensure that the cost is collected for the correct cost centre. Note the cost centre may also be a profit centre, in which case income would also be coded to it, or an investment centre, in which case assets, liabilities and capital may also be coded to it. For the moment however we shall just use the term cost centre for simplicity.

HOW IT WORKS

Wilmshurst Furniture Makers has three cost centres and has a management accounting coding system that uses a six digit code. All cost centre codes begin with the digits 01. The second two digits in the code then denote the precise cost centre to which the expense relates as follows:

- Cutting cost centre   01
- Assembly cost centre   02
- Polishing cost centre   03

The final two digits represent the type of cost:

- Materials   01
- Labour   02
- Expenses   03

The purchase invoice below was used and analysed in Chapter 2. We will now code each element of cost to show the type of cost – materials – and the cost centre to which they relate.

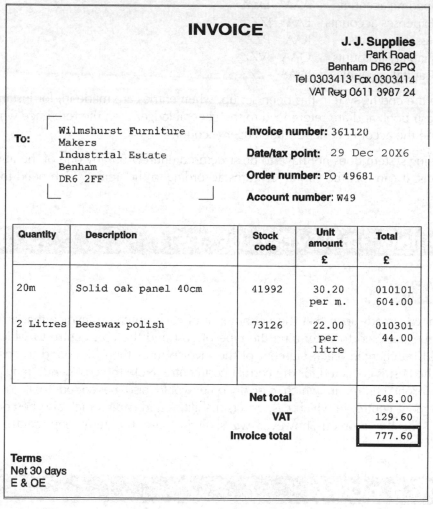

INVOICE

J. J. Supplies
Park Road
Benham DR6 2PQ
Tel 0303413 Fax 0303414
VAT Reg 0611 3987 24

To:
Wilmshurst Furniture Makers
Industrial Estate
Benham
DR6 2FF

Invoice number: 361120

Date/tax point: 29 Dec 20X6

Order number: PO 49681

Account number: W49

Quantity	Description	Stock code	Unit amount £	Total £
20m	Solid oak panel 40cm	41992	30.20 per m.	010101 604.00
2 Litres	Beeswax polish	73126	22.00 per litre	010301 44.00
		Net total		648.00
		VAT		129.60
		Invoice total		777.60

Terms
Net 30 days
E & OE

The solid oak panel is coded as follows:

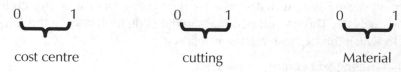

cost centre   cutting   Material

The polish is coded as:

cost centre	polishing	Material

Labour

The labour costs must also be coded. Remember that some elements of the labour cost may be charged as an expense or overhead rather than as direct labour.

HOW IT WORKS

Wilmshurst's policy is to charge any overtime premium as an expense together with the employer's NIC.

Remember Jim? In week 39 he worked for 29 hours in the cutting department and 12 hours in the assembly department for £378.40 in total. His six hours of overtime were due to the amount of work in the cutting department and the overtime premium part of this is to be treated as an expense or overhead rather than direct labour cost. The employer's NIC is calculated as £36.02.

His pay is analysed as follows:

	£
Cutting cost centre – labour cost 29 hours @ £8.60	249.40
Cutting cost centre – expense 6 hours @ £8.60 × 0.5	25.80
Cutting cost centre – expense NIC £36.02 × 29/41	25.48
Assembly cost centre – labour cost 12 hours @ £8.60	103.20
Assembly cost centre – expense NIC £36.02 × 12/41	10.54
Total cost/expense (£378.40 + £36.02)	414.42

This must now be coded:

Cutting cost centre – labour cost 29 hours @ £8.60	249.40 – 010102
Cutting cost centre – expense six hours @ £4.30	25.80 – 010103
Cutting cost centre – expense NIC £36.02 × 29/41	25.48 – 010103
Assembly cost centre – labour cost 12 hours @ £8.60	103.20 – 010202
Assembly cost centre – expense NIC £36.02 × 12/41	10.54 – 010203

The first two digits are always 01 as these are cost centres. The second pair of digits should be 01 for cutting and 02 for assembly. The final digits are 02 for the labour cost element and 03 for the expense or overhead element.

Task 1

Jan Simms works in the polishing department of Wilmshurst and has a 35-hour basic week with a basic time-rate of pay of £9.20 per hour and overtime paid at time-and-a-half. In week 32 she worked for 43 hours in total. The employer's NI is £42.55.

Show how the labour cost is made up and how it would be coded for this employee using the table below.

	Cost £	Code
Pay at basic time-rate		
Overtime premium		
Employer's NI		
Total cost		

Expenses

The expense or overhead costs must also be coded.

HOW IT WORKS

The factory rent and power costs were apportioned to the three production cost centres in Chapter 2 and must now be coded:

Factory rent –	Cutting	£3,000	–	010103
	Assembly	£2,000	–	010203
	Polishing	£1,000	–	010303
Factory power –	Cutting	£1,320	–	010103
	Assembly	£330	–	010203
	Polishing	£550	–	010303

The first two digits are 01 as these are cost centres. The second two digits represent the cost centre itself. The final two digits, 03, show that these are expenses or overheads.

Sales income

So far we have only concerned ourselves with costs. However, sales income or revenue must also be recognised in the management accounting records if the business operates profit centres (and/or investment centres). This is done by analysing the sales invoices to the correct profit centre and coding them appropriately.

HOW IT WORKS

Wilmshurst makes its sales through three outlets, in Dopham, Nutley and Jenson. The coding for sales is as follows:

First two digits	02 represents a profit centre	
Second two digits	Dopham profit centre	10
	Nutley profit centre	11
	Jenson profit centre	12
Third two digits	This depends upon the type of sale	
	– 5ft dining table	11
	– 6ft dining table	12
	– round coffee table	13
	– square coffee table	14
	– dining chair	15
	– 2-drawer chest	16
	– 3-drawer chest	17
	– 5ft wardrobe	18
	– 6ft wardrobe	19

Given below are two sales invoices that have to be coded.

INVOICE

Wilmshurst Furniture Makers
Retail Park
Jenson
DR2 4XK

To: Drayton Ltd

Invoice number: 42116

Date/tax point: 24 Dec 20X6

Order number: 62113

Account number: SL 47

Quantity	Description	Stock code	Unit amount £	Total £
2	6ft wardrobe	WR12	260.00	021219 520.00
1	6ft dining table	DT47	310.00	021212 310.00
8	Dining chair	DC06	56.00	021215 448.00
		Net total		1,278.00
		VAT		255.60
		Invoice total		1,533.60

Terms
Net 30 days
E & OE

INVOICE

Wilmshurst Furniture Makers
Retail Park
Nutley
DR5 2XJ

To: Hoopers Stores Ltd

Invoice number: 42117

Date/tax point: 24 Dec 20X6

Order number: 24 Dec 20X6

Account number: SL 02

Quantity	Description	Stock code	Unit amount £	Total £
8	Round coffee table	RC11	130.00	021113 1,040.00
6	Round coffee table	CD03	210.00	021117 1,260.00
6	3-drawer chest	CD02	160.00	021116 960.00
		Net total		3,260.00
		VAT		652.00
		Invoice total		3,912.00

Terms
Net 30 days
E & OE

The coding of each item is:

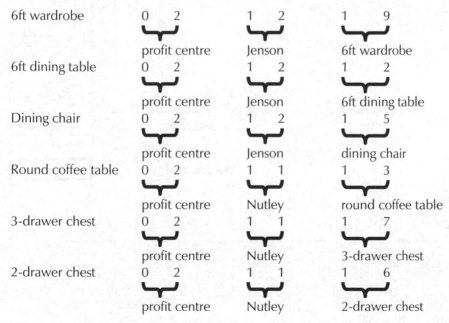

	profit centre	Jenson	6ft wardrobe
6ft wardrobe	0 2	1 2	1 9
6ft dining table	0 2 (profit centre)	1 2 (Jenson)	1 2 (6ft dining table)
Dining chair	0 2 (profit centre)	1 2 (Jenson)	1 5 (dining chair)
Round coffee table	0 2 (profit centre)	1 1 (Nutley)	1 3 (round coffee table)
3-drawer chest	0 2 (profit centre)	1 1 (Nutley)	1 7 (3-drawer chest)
2-drawer chest	0 2 (profit centre)	1 1 (Nutley)	1 6 (2-drawer chest)

Task 2

Given below is a further sales invoice for Wilmshurst. Enter the correct coding on the invoice in the boxes given.

INVOICE

Wilmshurst Furniture Makers
Retail Park
Dopham
DR3 4ZJ

To: Bots & Co

Invoice number: 42118

Date/tax point: 5 Dec 20X6

Order number: P04662

Account number: SL 17

Quantity	Description	Stock code	Unit amount £	Total £
6	Dining chair	DC08	56.00	336.00
1	5ft dining table	DT31	270.00	270.00
	Net total			606.00
	VAT			121.20
	Invoice total			727.20

Terms
Net 30 days
E & OE

UPDATING COST, PROFIT AND INVESTMENT CENTRE BALANCES

Once the invoices and payroll details have been analysed and coded, the amounts to be charged for each cost to each cost centre, the income to be credited to a profit centre, and the assets/liabilities/capital to be recorded as belonging to an investment centre must be added to the current balance for each account. This will give the total to date for each cost/profit/investment centre and each type of cost/income/asset/liability/capital.

HOW IT WORKS

All of the costs coded for Wilmshurst in this chapter so far (excluding the task) are now summarised below:

Code	£
010101	604.00
010102	249.40
010103	25.80
010103	25.48
010103	3,000.00
010103	1,320.00
010202	103.20
010203	10.54
010203	2,000.00
010203	330.00
010301	44.00
010303	1,000.00
010303	550.00

An extract from the cost centre list of balances is also given. Each balance must be updated using the figures above to show the total for each cost.

Code	Opening balance	Update	Closing balance 31 Dec 20X6
	£	£	£
010101	37,886.98		
010102	86,779.20		
010103	23,556.90		
010201	9,667.23		
010202	93,674.55		
010203	25,634.01		
010301	10,356.35		
010302	68,362.00		
010303	12,563.98		

Step 1 Find the total cost to be added to each code.

Code	£	
010101	604.00	£604.00
010102	249.40	£249.40
010103	25.80	
010103	25.48	£4,371.28
010103	3,000.00	
010103	1,320.00	
010202	103.20	£103.20
010203	10.54	
010203	2,000.00	£2,340.54
010203	330.00	
010301	44.00	£44.00
010303	1,000.00	
010303	550.00	£1,550.00

Step 2 Enter the new costs coded above into the update column to be added into the opening balance.

Code	Opening balance	Update	Closing balance 31 Dec 20X6
	£	£	£
010101	37,886.98	604.00	
010102	86,779.20	249.40	
010103	23,556.90	4,371.28	
010201	9,667.23		
010202	93,674.55	103.20	
010203	25,634.01	2,340.54	
010301	10,356.35	44.00	
010302	68,362.00		
010303	12,563.98	1,550.00	

Step 3 Total the opening balance and the new costs to find the closing balance.

Code	Opening balance	Update	Closing balance 31 Dec 20X6
	£	£	£
010101	37,886.98	604.00	38,490.98
010102	86,779.20	249.40	87,028.60
010103	23,556.90	4,371.28	27,928.18
010201	9,667.23		9,667.23
010202	93,674.55	103.20	93,777.75
010203	25,634.01	2,340.54	27,974.55
010301	10,356.35	44.00	10,400.35
010302	68,362.00		68,362.00
010303	12,563.98	1,550.00	14,113.98

Task 3

Given below is a summary of all of the income coded in Wilmhurst's accounts this week:

021113	1,040		
021116	960		
021117	1,260		
021212	310		
021215	448		
021219	520		

You are also given the opening balances on the profit centre accounts:

Code	Opening balance £	Update £	Closing balance 31 Dec 20X6 £
021113	21,056		
021116	96,100		
021117	22,650		
021212	53,682		
021215	3,480		
021219	12,420		

Enter the new income into the update column and find the closing balance on each of the profit centre accounts.

CHAPTER OVERVIEW

- There are many methods of coding and each business will devise its own system.

- Each purchase invoice is analysed and coded as to the type of cost (materials or expense) and the cost centre (or profit or investment centre) that it relates to.

- The payroll details are also coded to indicate the elements of gross pay that are treated as labour and the elements treated as an expense, and the cost centres etc they relate to.

- The expenses are coded to show the cost centre they relate to.

- Sales invoices are analysed to indicate the profit centre they relate to and in some systems also the product that is being sold.

- In some systems assets, liabilities and capital can be coded for the investment centre to which they relate.

- Once all of the costs and income have been collected for a period then the balance in the cost/profit/investment centre account is updated to show the additional costs/income collected for that centre.

Keywords

Numeric coding – a coding system that uses numbers only

Alpha-numeric coding – a coding system that uses letters and numbers

Alphabetic coding – a coding system that uses just letters

TEST YOUR LEARNING

Test 1

Pole Potteries has a three-digit coding system for its cost centres:

Digit one	1	**means that this is a cost centre**	
Digit two		denotes the actual cost centre:	
	–	throwing	1
	–	baking	2
	–	painting	3
	–	packaging	4
	–	stores	5
	–	maintenance	6
	–	selling and distribution	7
	–	canteen	8
	–	administration	9
Digit three		denotes the type of cost:	
	–	materials	1
	–	labour	2
	–	expenses	3

Code the following purchase invoices using the three-digit coding system above. Enter your answers into the boxes on the invoices below.

INVOICE

Purbeck Clay
Granite Yard
Compston BH3 4TL
Tel 01929 464810
VAT Reg 1164 2810 67

To: Pole Potteries

Invoice number: 36411

Date/tax point: 16 Dec 20X6

Order number: 11663

Account number: SL 42

Quantity	Description	Stock code	Unit amount £	Total £
50 kg	Throwing clay	TC412	6.80	340.00
10 litres	Paint - Fuchsia	PF67	2.80	28.00
		Net total		368.00
		VAT		73.60
		Invoice total		441.60

Terms
Net 30 days
E & OE

INVOICE

IndCan Suppliers
High Street
Hamware BH3 7SP
Tel 01929 432432
VAT Reg 2214 6182 93

To: Pole Potteries

Invoice number: 61212

Date/tax point: 17 Dec 20X6

Order number: 11668

Account number: PP 02

Quantity	Description	Stock code	Unit amount £	Total £
100 kg	Frozen chips	46112	1.20	120.00
48	Chicken pies	61297	0.90	43.20

Net total	163.20
VAT	32.64
Invoice total	195.84

Terms
Net 30 days
E & OE

Test 2

Remember Lara Binns who works for Pole Potteries? Her gross pay for week 39 has been analysed so that the overtime premium can be treated as an expense as follows:

	£	Code
Throwing – labour 26 hours @ £9.60 =	249.60	
Baking – labour 15 hours @ £9.60 =	144.00	
Throwing – expense – overtime premium 3 × 9.60 =	28.80	
Throwing – expense – employer's NIC	26.42	
Baking – expense – employer's NIC	15.25	

Use the coding system in Test 1 to code Lara's pay correctly, entering the code in the box next to each description.

Test 3

The expenses of Pole Potteries for the period have been analysed and summarised below. Use the coding system to code these too.

	£	Code
Throwing – expense – rent £15,000 × 15%	2,250	
Throwing – expense – cleaning	200	
Throwing – total	2,450	
Baking – expense – rent £15,000 × 40%	6,000	
Baking – expense – servicing	600	
Baking – total	6,600	
Painting – expense – rent £15,000 × 15%	2,250	
Packaging – expense – rent £5,000 × 20%	1,000	
Stores – expense – rent £5,000 × 80%	4,000	
Maintenance – expense – rent £15,000 × 10%	1,500	
Selling and distribution – expense – rent £3,000 × 0.5	1,500	
Selling and distribution – expense – advertising	400	
Selling and distribution – total	1,900	
Canteen – expense – rent £15,000 × 20%	3,000	
Administration – expense – rent £3,000 × 0.5	1,500	

Test 4

A manufacturer of washing machines uses a numerical coding structure based on one profit centre and three cost centres as outlined below. Each code has a sub-code so each transaction will be coded as */**.

Profit/Cost Centre	Code	Sub-classification	Sub-code
Sales	1	UK Sales	10
		EU Sales	20
Production	2	Direct Cost	10
		Indirect Cost	20
Selling and Distribution	3	Direct Cost	10
		Indirect Cost	20
Administration	4	Direct Cost	10
		Indirect Cost	20

Code the following revenue and expense transactions that have been extracted from purchase invoices, sales invoices and the payroll, using the table below.

Transaction	Code
Materials for casings	
Sales to Paris, EU	
Business rates on factory	
Sales commission paid	
Sales to Holmfirth, UK	
Office stationery	

chapter 7:
COMPARISON OF COSTS AND INCOME

---

chapter coverage 📖

In this chapter we consider comparing the actual cost and income information collected to expected figures in order to provide useful information for management. The topics covered are:

- ✍ Comparison of actual with expected results
- ✍ The budget
- ✍ Comparing actual with budget: variances
- ✍ Calculation of variances
- ✍ Reporting of variances
- ✍ Using spreadsheets
- ✍ Entering data into a spreadsheet
- ✍ Entering basic formulae into a spreadsheet
- ✍ Calculating percentages in a spreadsheet
- ✍ Calculating averages in a spreadsheet
- ✍ Reorganising data in a spreadsheet
- ✍ Presenting a spreadsheet

COMPARISON OF ACTUAL WITH EXPECTED RESULTS

In the first chapter we considered the role of management in an organisation and that one of the key elements of this role was control. One way in which the costs and income of an organisation can be controlled is by comparing actual results with expected results as set out in the organisation's budget.

Deciding on what we expect to be the income and cost figures for a future period is a complex process which you will learn more about later in your studies. Many organisations have what is known as a STANDARD COST for items they produce, setting out what they expect each unit to cost in terms of materials and labour. This standard cost is then multiplied by the number of items expected to be produced in order to estimate expected figures. Some organisations also have a standard for the selling price that they use in the calculations of income.

THE BUDGET

The BUDGET of a business is its formal financial plan. The budget is determined for a future period and shows the expected levels of production and sales and the expected (or standard) costs and income associated with the production and sales levels.

Budgets are normally prepared on a monthly basis, so for each month's actual figures there will be budgeted or expected figures to compare with. The organisation as a whole is likely to have a budget for at least one year ahead, which is updated and reviewed regularly.

Included in the budget will be:

- BUDGETED INCOME, which is the amount of income or revenue the business expects to generate in sales of products, calculated as:

  Expected units sold x Expected (or standard) selling price per unit

- BUDGETED COSTS, which are the expected amounts of expenditure on direct costs (materials and labour) and overheads (indirect materials and labour, plus expenses)

- BUDGETED PROFIT, which is calculated as:

  Budgeted income – budgeted costs

COMPARING ACTUAL WITH BUDGET: VARIANCES

Comparison of expected figures with actual results is an extremely important tool for management in their control of the business. The differences between the actual costs and income and the budgeted costs and income are known as VARIANCES. These can be adverse ('bad' for the business) or favourable ('good' for the business).

Any significant variances should be reported to management, as a priority, as the reasons for them must be investigated and corrective action taken.

CALCULATION OF VARIANCES

Adverse and favourable variances

ADVERSE VARIANCE – Where it is bad or negative for the business because:

- the actual cost is greater than the budgeted cost, or

- the actual income is less than the budgeted income

FAVOURABLE VARIANCE – Where it is good or positive for the business because:

- the actual cost is less than budgeted cost, or

- the actual income is greater than budgeted income

Significant variances

Whether a variance is significant depends on the context of the organisation.

Managers will want to be aware of significant variances, whether they are adverse or favourable. You might think that they are only concerned with adverse variances but a favourable variance may be an indication of a job well done by a department manager or the fact that the budget was not a fair reflection of the cost or income expected.

HOW IT WORKS

We have Wilmshurst's cost centre costs for December 20X6 from Chapter 6.

Code	Opening balance	Update	Closing balance 31 Dec 20X6
	£	£	£
010101	37,886.98	604.00	38,490.98
010102	86,779.20	249.40	87,028.60
010103	23,556.90	4,371.28	27,928.18
010201	9,667.23		9,667.23
010202	93,674.55	103.20	93,777.75
010203	25,634.01	2,340.54	27,974.55
010301	10,356.35	44.00	10,400.35
010302	68,362.00		68,362.00
010303	12,563.98	1,550.00	14,113.98

From the budget, the expected costs for December 20X6 were as follows:

Budgeted costs – production cost centres – December 20X6

Code	£
010101	37,200.00
010102	86,770.00
010103	23,550.00
010201	9,600.00
010202	99,540.00
010203	32,600.00
010301	10,350.00
010302	74,300.00
010303	10,560.00

Now we need to compare the actual costs with the expected costs and to calculate the variances. This is done simply by deducting the actual figure from the budgeted figure.

Comparison of actual cost with budgeted cost for December 20X6

		Actual £	Budget £	Variance £
Cutting –	materials	38,490.98	37,200.00	-1,290.98 A
	labour	87,028.60	86,770.00	-258.60 A
	expenses	27,928.18	23,550.00	-4,378.18 A
Assembly –	materials	9,667.23	9,600.00	-67.23 A
	labour	93,777.75	99,540.00	5,762.25 F
	expenses	27,974.55	32,600.00	4,625.45 F
Polishing –	materials	10,400.35	10,350.00	-50.35 A
	labour	68,362.00	74,300.00	5,938.00 F
	expenses	14,113.98	10,560.00	-3,553.98 A

As these are all cost variances, it follows that:

- a negative result from deducting actual cost from budget is bad for the business – more cost has been incurred than planned. We can therefore classify such a result as adverse (A).

- a positive result is good for the business as it means less cost has been incurred than planned, so this is favourable (F).

Comparison of actual income with budgeted income

If we were dealing with income, the situation would be reversed.

- a positive result from deducting actual income from budgeted income is bad for the business, as less actual income has been generated than budgeted. This would be classified as adverse (A)

- a negative result is good for the business as it means more income has been generated than planned, so this is favourable (F)

Task 1

Given below is the actual income for each of Wilmshurst's profit centres for December 20X6 and the budgeted income for the month.

	Actual income month of December 20X6 £
Dopham	185,213
Nutley	167,232
Jenson	113,415

	Budgeted income month of December 20X6 £
Dopham	175,000
Nutley	170,000
Jenson	120,000

Compare the actual and budgeted figures and calculate the variances, indicating whether each one is adverse or favourable. Then calculate what percentage of the budgeted amount each variance is. Use the table below for your answer.

Profit centre	Actual income Dec 20X6 £	Budgeted income Dec 20X6 £	Variance £	Adverse (A) or Favourable (F)	Variance as % of budgeted income
Dopham					
Nutley					
Jenson					

REPORTING OF VARIANCES

Normally the managers of a business only wish to be informed about significant variances, by means of a VARIANCE REPORT or SIGNIFICANCE REPORT.

The significance of a variance cannot be determined simply by its size – the size of the variance must be compared with the budgeted amount. For example a variance of £10,000 is tiny if the budgeted amount is £1,000,000 but is huge if the budgeted amount is only £15,000.

Therefore the significance of a variance will often be determined by measuring it as a percentage of the budgeted figure. If it is more than, say, 10% of the budgeted amount then the organisation's policy may be that it must be reported to management.

HOW IT WORKS

We will now calculate the percentage that each variance is of the **budgeted** amount. Note that:

- it is calculated relative to the budgeted or expected amount, NOT the actual amount

- you can ignore any minus sign as it is the relative size of the figures that are key here

Cutting –	materials	1,290.98/37,200	×	100	=	3.5% A
	labour	258.60/86,770	×	100	=	0.3% A
	expenses	4,378.18/23,550	×	100	=	18.6% A
Assembly –	materials	67.23/9,600	×	100	=	0.7% A
	labour	5,762.25/99,540	×	100	=	5.8% F
	expenses	4,625.45/32,600	×	100	=	14.2% F
Polishing –	materials	50.35/10,350	×	100	=	0.5% A
	labour	5,938.00/74,300	×	100	=	8.0% F
	expenses	3,553.98/10,560	×	100	=	33.7% A

If Wilmshurst's policy is to report any variances over 5% of the budgeted amount then the following would be reported:

Cutting	expenses	£4,378.18 Adverse
Assembly	labour	£5,762.25 Favourable
	expenses	£4,625.45 Favourable
Polishing	labour	£5,938.00 Favourable
	expenses	£3,553.98 Adverse

If the policy had been to report only variances greater than 10% of budget then the only variances reported would have been the three expenses variances.

USING SPREADSHEETS

So far in this chapter we have covered the information contained in an organisation's budget and how that information is used to calculate variances from actual results, identifying each one as either a bad consequence for the business (adverse) or a good consequence for the business (favourable). We have also looked at calculating variances as percentages of budget to establish whether they should be reported as significant to management.

If you are familiar at all with spreadsheets it may have occurred to you that they would prove a useful tool in calculating and presenting information. You may already have come across spreadsheets at college, at home or at work. Nearly all PCs have spreadsheet software, typically Excel, preloaded.

A SPREADSHEET is a computer application which allows the user to record, calculate, organise and analyse numerical data in tables. It can be used:

- To make large numbers of calculations very rapidly, provided the correct data and formulae are entered

- To format and present information in a clear and user-friendly way

For these reasons using spreadsheets is a key area of the Basic Costing unit in the context of making comparisons of income and expenditure data.

ENTERING DATA INTO A SPREADSHEET

A spreadsheet is presented in the form of a table or grid, with rows and columns. Typically a WORKSHEET in a spreadsheet (each spreadsheet can have any number of worksheets, rather like a book can have any number of pages) will appear initially as follows:

	A	B	C	D	E	F
1						
2						
3						
4						
5						

Let's look at the basics of how a spreadsheet works:

- The top row (greyed out) is pre-set in the spreadsheet and shows the references to its columns, in this case columns A to F. The top row cannot be altered by the user

- The left hand column (again greyed out) is also pre-set in the spreadsheet and shows the references to its rows, in this case rows 1 to 5. This column cannot be altered by the user

- Each 'box' in the body of the spreadsheet is called a CELL, and each cell has a reference which denotes its position, being the intersection of a row and column. For instance the cell where column A and row 1 intersect has the cell reference A1, whereas where column E and row 3 intersect the cell reference is E3. All the cell references for this spreadsheet are shown below (they are not usually visible on the spreadsheet):

	A	B	C	D	E	F
1	A1	B1	C1	D1	E1	F1
2	A2	B2	C2	D2	E2	F2
3	A3	B3	C3	D3	E3	F3
4	A4	B4	C4	D4	E4	F4
5	A5	B5	C5	D5	E5	F5

- Each cell is an active part of the spreadsheet, which can be:

  - Entered with data ie a number, or letters (text), or

  - Entered with a formula which will operate on other cells to generate a number (or text), and

  - Formatted so that it presents the information in the desired way

HOW IT WORKS

We will enter the variance information that we saw in the answer to Task 1 related to Wilmshurst's profit centres in December 20X6 into the spreadsheet.

- In Row 1 we will enter 'header' information as text so that the user can see what the data in each column relates to, that is Profit centre (see cell A1 for column 1) in column A, Actual income (B1) in column B, and Budgeted income (C1) in column C. Note that cells B1 and C1 also contain £ signs, to denote that the numbers in those columns refer to money, rather than to (say) the number of units sold

- Column A contains 'header' information as text about which profit centre the data in each row refers to, that is Dopham (A2 for row 2), Nutley (A3 for row 3) and Jenson (A4 for row 4)

- Column B cells B2 to B4 contain the numerical data for actual income for each profit centre

- Column C cells C2 to C4 contain the numerical data for budgeted income for each profit centre

	A	B	C	D	E	F
1	Profit centre	Actual income £	Budgeted income £			
2	Dopham	185,213	175,000			
3	Nutley	167,232	170,000			
4	Jenson	113,415	120,000			
5						

ENTERING BASIC FORMULAE INTO A SPREADSHEET

Spreadsheets are a very useful means of recording numerical data and presenting them as information. It would be possible for managers just to use the spreadsheet above as a record of the data, as it contains the data needed and presents it in a neat way. However the real benefit of spreadsheets is that we can – if we choose – get them to make calculations for us. We do this by entering a FORMULA in relevant cells so that the figure that appears in that cell is the result of doing something to one or more of the numbers in the other cells.

The formulae that we need to cover for Basic Costing are:

Add:	=(B1+B2)
Subtract:	=(B1–B2)
Multiply:	=(B1*B2)
Divide:	=(B1/B2)
Total:	=SUM(B1:B2)
Average:	=AVERAGE(B1:B2)

Note that:

- There should be no spaces within any formula
- All formulae are preceded by an = sign
- All cell references are contained within brackets
- The multiplication sign is the asterisk (*), not an x or X

Subtraction

Let's start with subtraction.

HOW IT WORKS

For Wilmshurst we want to calculate the amount of the variance between the actual income and the budgeted income for each profit centre. To do this we first of all enter 'Variance £' as the header for column D in cell D1.

	A	B	C	D	E	F
1	Profit centre	Actual income £	Budgeted income £	Variance £		
2	Dopham	185,213	175,000			
3	Nutley	167,232	170,000			
4	Jenson	113,415	120,000			
5						

We then potentially have two options:

- Calculate each variance on a calculator and enter the answer as numbers in cells D2 to D4, or

- Enter a formula in cells D2 to D4 so that the spreadsheet can make the calculation for us by subtracting one cell from the other

To make full use of the spreadsheet's abilities we shall use a formula, based on subtracting the actual income from budgeted income as before. For Dopham the calculation and formula are:

Calculation: $175,000 - 185,213$ $= -10,213$

Formula: $=(C2-B2)$

The formulae are added to each of cells D2 to D4 as follows:

	A	B	C	D	E	F
1	Profit centre	Actual income £	Budgeted income £	Variance £		
2	Dopham	185,213	175,000	=(C2–B2)		
3	Nutley	167,232	170,000	=(C3–B3)		
4	Jenson	113,415	120,000	=(C4–B4)		
5						

Although what you have keyed in to the spreadsheet is the formula, what will actually appear is the number you were looking for, as the spreadsheet calculates the number and presents it for you:

	A	B	C	D	E	F
1	Profit centre	Actual income £	Budgeted income £	Variance £		
2	Dopham	185,213	175,000	-10,213		
3	Nutley	167,232	170,000	2,768		
4	Jenson	113,415	120,000	6,585		
5						

Having calculated the amounts of the variances, we can identify whether each one is adverse or favourable by using column E and entering the column header (no £ sign is necessary) then A or F as relevant. Remember that, as before, an adverse variance is what is bad for the business; clearly the shortfall in actual income from budgeted income for Nutley and Jenson is bad for business and must be denoted A. **Do not be distracted by the fact these figures come out as positive rather than negative on the spreadsheet; you need to think carefully about what each one actually means**.

	A	B	C	D	E	F
1	Profit centre	Actual income £	Budgeted income £	Variance £	Adverse (A)/Favourable (F)	
2	Dopham	185,213	175,000	-10,213	F	
3	Nutley	167,232	170,000	2,768	A	
4	Jenson	113,415	120,000	6,585	A	
5						

Addition, multiplication and division

The same principles apply for these three basic functions as apply to subtraction. Have a go at Task 2 to see how it works.

Task 2

(a) What formulae would you enter in cells B5 and C5 if you wanted these to be the total figures for the three cells above each one?

B5 [   ]

C5 [   ]

(b) What formulae would you enter in cells B5 and C5 if you wanted these to be the result of multiplying together the amounts in the two cells above each one?

B5 [   ]

C5 [   ]

(c) What formula would you enter in cell F2 if you wanted this to be the result of dividing Dopham's budgeted income by its actual income?

F2 [   ]

Auto-sum (total)

Very often in a spreadsheet there is a long column or row of figures that requires a total. It would be very tedious if we had to key in a long formula for this in the format =(B2+B3+B4+...) etc, although it could be done like that as we saw in part (a) of Task 2. Instead there is a formula you can enter that allows you to total, or AUTO-SUM, two or more cells.

Auto-sum or Total: =SUM(B1:B2)

HOW IT WORKS

Suppose we wanted to calculate Wilmshurst's total actual income for December 20X6. The relevant figures are contained in cells B2, B3 and B4, and we would like to present the total figure in cell B5. We would therefore enter the auto-sum formula, which in this case is =SUM(B2:B4). The result would show as 465,860:

	A	B	C	D	E	F
1	Profit centre	Actual income £	Budgeted income £	Variance £	Adverse (A)/ Favourable (F)	
2	Dopham	185,213	175,000	-10,213	F	
3	Nutley	167,232	170,000	2,768	A	
4	Jenson	113,415	120,000	6,585	A	
5	Total	=SUM(B2:B4) 465,860				

In most spreadsheet packages there is an automatic button that can be used for auto-summing. The button is the Greek letter 'sigma' and looks like this:

$$\sum$$

When you click this button the spreadsheet automatically selects which cells should be included in the sum – generally these are the ones either in the column above, or in the row to the side. To accept this selection you just press the RETURN KEY on the keyboard:

To amend the selection presented by the spreadsheet, you key in different cell references to the formula presented by the spreadsheet.

CALCULATING PERCENTAGES IN A SPREADSHEET

We have already seen, when looking at variances, that calculating a percentage is a useful way of assessing whether there is something significant about the comparison between two figures. Again spreadsheets can help with this, but to do so you need to appreciate something about formatting cells in a spreadsheet.

Formatting cells

The FORMAT of a cell determines how the cell is displayed, for instance:

- as a basic or 'general' number (10)
- as a monetary amount (£10)
- as a percentage (10%)
- as a figure to only two decimals (10.00)

Cells in a spreadsheet have a default format of 'general' which means that:

- If you key numbers or letters into the cell without an = sign, you will see the numbers or letters in the cell as you keyed them

- If you key a formula into the cell preceded by an = sign, you will see the result of that formula

However it is possible to format the cell instead to present the result in some other way. For our purposes the format that is useful is PERCENTAGE, which means to express one figure in terms of another.

HOW IT WORKS

We want to calculate the variance for each of the rows on Wilmshurst's spreadsheet as a percentage of the budgeted income figure. We could simply use a calculator and enter the figure into the relevant cell, or we could use the spreadsheet to do this for us. A two-step process is required to do this:

Step 1:   In column F enter the formula that calculates the variance as a percentage of budgeted income, which is Variance/Budgeted income ie (in the case of Dopham) =(D2/C2). Just entering this formula will produce the following result, which is a decimal rather than a percentage:

	A	B	C	D	E	F
1	Profit centre	Actual income £	Budgeted income £	Variance £	Adverse (A)/ Favourable (F)	Variance as % of budgeted income
2	Dopham	185,213	175,000	-10,213	F	=(D2/C2) 0.05836
3	Nutley	167,232	170,000	2,768	A	=(D3/C3) 0.01628
4	Jenson	113,415	120,000	6,585	A	=(D4/C4) 0.05487
5	Total	465,860				

Step 2: Tell the spreadsheet to format the three cells as 'Percentage' (you do not need to be able to actually do this in the assessment). The spreadsheet will then convert each of the decimals into a number with '%' after it:

	A	B	C	D	E	F
1	Profit centre	Actual income £	Budgeted income £	Variance £	Adverse (A)/ Favourable (F)	Variance as % of budgeted income
2	Dopham	185,213	175,000	-10,213	F	5.8%
3	Nutley	167,232	170,000	2,768	A	1.6%
4	Jenson	113,415	120,000	6,585	A	5.5%
5	Total	465,860				

Note that to have a percentage rounded to one decimal place as seen above there is some further formatting to do which is beyond the scope of this assessment. Again you do not need to be able to actually do this in the assessment.

CALCULATING AVERAGES IN A SPREADSHEET

There is one further calculation that is made more accurate, clearer and simpler by using a spreadsheet, and that is calculating an AVERAGE of two of more figures. There may be a number of circumstances when this would prove useful, for example calculating:

- The average income of a number of profit centres
- The average wage of a number of employees
- The average cost of a number of different products.

To calculate an average in a spreadsheet you need to insert a formula into the relevant cell:

Average: =AVERAGE(B1:B2)

HOW IT WORKS

Suppose Wilmshurst wanted to present the average actual income of its three profit centres in its spreadsheet. It could do this in two ways:

- Add up the three figures for actual income in cells B2, B3 and B4 and divide by the number of profit centres, that is 3, and enter the result (155,287) in cell B5

- Enter the relevant formula in cell B5, which is =AVERAGE(B2:B4)

	A	B	C	D	E	F
1	Profit centre	Actual income £	Budgeted income £	Variance £	Adverse (A)/ Favourable (F)	Variance as % of budgeted income
2	Dopham	185,213	175,000	-10,213	F	5.8%
3	Nutley	167,232	170,000	2,768	A	1.6%
4	Jenson	113,415	120,000	6,585	A	5.5%
5	Average	=AVERAGE(B2:B4) 155,287				

REORGANISING DATA IN A SPREADSHEET

The final way in which you need to use spreadsheets to provide information in this unit is in reorganising data so that it is more useful to the users, who will generally be the organisation's managers in the case of actual and budgeted income and expenditure. This can be done in a number of ways, such as alphabetically and numerically.

For instance you may have a spreadsheet of account data, each row including account name, account balance (in £) and numerical code. You could choose to order the rows of the spreadsheet:

- in account name order alphabetically, ascending from A to Z or (if you really felt like it!) descending from Z to A

- in account number order numerically, ascending from lowest to highest number or descending from highest to lowest number

- in order of the size of the balances numerically, again ascending from lowest to highest number or descending from highest to lowest number

The point to remember is that for the information to remain useful, you are not just reordering the data in one column, you are reordering all the data, so the right account balance and code stay with the right name for instance.

HOW IT WORKS

Suppose Wilmshurst's managers wanted to see the information you have prepared in the order of the lowest variance as a percentage of budget to the highest, that is in ascending numerical order with respect to column F. You would have to re-order rows 2 to 4 of the spreadsheet from this...

	A	B	C	D	E	F
1	Profit centre	Actual income £	Budgeted income £	Variance £	Adverse (A)/ Favourable (F)	Variance as % of budgeted income
2	Dopham	185,213	175,000	-10,213	F	5.8%
3	Nutley	167,232	170,000	2,768	A	1.6%
4	Jenson	113,415	120,000	6,585	A	5.5%

...to this:

	A	B	C	D	E	F
1	Profit centre	Actual income £	Budgeted income £	Variance £	Adverse (A)/ Favourable (F)	Variance as % of budgeted income
2	Nutley	167,232	170,000	2,768	A	1.6%
3	Jenson	113,415	120,000	6,585	A	5.5%
4	Dopham	185,213	175,000	-10,213	F	5.8%

In a spreadsheet you could do this just by highlighting the cells that you wish to re-order (cells A2 to F4 – do not include the header row) and pressing one of two SORT BUTTONS:

- To change to ascending order (sort smallest to largest) use this button:

A
Z
Sort

- To change to descending order (sort largest to smallest) use this button:

Z
A
Sort

When the button is pressed the spreadsheet asks which column it should use to make the sorting, eg column D to sort by size of variance.

PRESENTING A SPREADSHEET

Many organisations have policies on how spreadsheets should be presented visually, for instance as regards colours, fonts etc. In general however the principles to be followed when preparing information in a spreadsheet for presentation to users are as follows:

- Save the spreadsheet to your PC securely and keep a backup

- Use a password when saving the spreadsheet to protect the information if it is confidential (as it is likely to be where it contains financial data)

- Name the spreadsheet as a whole, and each worksheet within it, clearly

- Make sure there is enough space in the cells for the information contained in them – you can size the rows and columns as you wish

- Consider the order of the columns and rows carefully, paying attention to the same conventions we have seen throughout your studies so far, such as having totals for columns of figures at the bottom of the column rather than at the top

- Make sure the headers for columns and rows are clear and relate to the data you insert

- Consider using colour to highlight key pieces of information in the spreadsheet

- Carefully check the spreadsheet in its final form:

    - Check that you have entered numbers correctly
    - Check that the formulae you have used relate to the correct cells
    - Check that you have not made any spelling errors

CHAPTER OVERVIEW

- One of the key roles of management is control – this can be helped by constant comparison of actual results with expected or budgeted figures.

- A key element in management control of a business is the budget – actual results should be compared with the expected or budgeted figures and the differences, called variances, reported to management when significant.

- It is important that both adverse and favourable variances are reported on a significance basis, as a percentage of the budgeted figure.

- Spreadsheets can be used to help in both calculating figures and presenting them clearly to managers

Keywords

Standard cost – an estimate of materials and labour cost per unit to use when developing an estimate of future results

Budget – formalised financial plan of the future operations of the organisation

Budgeted income – expected sales in units multiplied by expected sales price per unit

Budgeted costs – expected amounts of expenditure (materials, labour and expenses)

Budgeted profit – budgeted income less budgeted costs

Variances – the difference between the expected or budgeted cost/income and the actual cost/income

Adverse variance – the actual result is worse for the business than the budgeted result

Favourable variance – the actual result is better for the business than the budgeted result

Variance report or **significance report** – a report to an appropriate person of significant variances between actual and budget, usually identified as being above a certain percentage of budget

Spreadsheet - a computer application which allows the user to record, calculate, organise and analyse numerical data in tables

Worksheet – a page of a spreadsheet, consisting of a table or grid of cells

Cell – an active part of the spreadsheet in which numbers, text or formulae can be entered by the user

Keywords cont'd

Formula – text entered in a spreadsheet cell which, by reference to one or more other cells, results in a calculation being made and presented

Auto-sum – a spreadsheet formula that totals the figures covered by the formula: =SUM(A1:A2) etc

Return key – the key on the computer keyboard which tells the spreadsheet to accept the data or formula that you have entered

Format – of a spreadsheet cell determines how the cell is displayed, eg as a general number, a monetary amount, a percentage or a figure to one or more decimals

Percentage – expressing one number in terms of another

Average – a spreadsheet formula that calculates a numerical average of the amounts in question, by totalling the amounts and dividing by the number of amounts: =AVERAGE(A1:A2)

Sort button – a facility available in the spreadsheet package to re-order data in either ascending or descending order

TEST YOUR LEARNING

Test 1

Given below are the actual costs of the production cost centres for Pole Potteries for November 20X6.

		£
Throwing –	materials	12,140
	labour	7,440
	expenses	6,330
Baking –	materials	1,330
	labour	2,440
	expenses	10,490
Painting –	materials	4,260
	labour	13,570
	expenses	2,680

Here are the budgeted costs for the production cost centres for Pole Potteries for November 20X6.

		£
Throwing –	materials	11,200
	labour	6,150
	expenses	7,130
Baking –	materials	1,500
	labour	2,490
	expenses	11,350
Painting –	materials	3,660
	labour	11,240
	expenses	2,800

Produce a comparison of actual costs for November 20X6 with budgeted costs for the month and show the amount of the variances and whether each one is adverse (A) or favourable (F). Fill in your answers in the table below. The policy of Pole Potteries is to report any variances that are more than 10% of the budgeted amount to management. Calculate the variance as a percentage of budget for each cost. Enter your answers in the second table below.

	Actual £	Budget £	Variance £
Throwing			
Materials			
Labour			
Expenses			
Baking			
Materials			
Labour			
Expenses			
Painting			
Materials			
Labour			
Expenses			

Cost centre	Expense	Variance £	Variance as a % of budget
Throwing	Materials		
	Labour		
	Expenses		
Baking	Materials		
	Labour		
	Expenses		
Painting	Materials		
	Labour		
	Expenses		

Test 2

Identify the following statements as being True or False by putting a tick in the relevant column of the table below.

	True	False
The difference between a budgeted and an actual cost is called performance		
An adverse variance occurs when actual income exceeds budgeted income		

Test 3

A business has produced a variance report detailing budgeted and actual costs for the month. Calculate the variance for each cost type and then determine whether it is adverse or favourable by putting a tick in the relevant column of the table below.

Cost type	Budget £	Actual £	Variance £	Adverse	Favourable
Direct materials	52,480	51,940			
Direct labour	65,920	67,370			
Production overheads	34,340	35,680			
Selling and distribution overheads	10,270	12,840			
Administration overheads	11,560	10,470			

Test 4

The following variance report for a particular month has been produced for a business. Any variance in excess of 5% of budget is deemed to be significant and should be reported to management.

Calculate the variances in the table below as a percentage of the budgeted figure and indicate whether they are significant or not by putting a tick in the relevant column.

Cost type	Budget £	Variance £	Adverse/ Favourable	Variance as a % of budget	Significant	Not Significant
Direct materials	134,280	20,390	Favourable			
Direct labour	128,410	5,400	Adverse			
Production overheads	87,360	9,280	Adverse			
Selling and distribution overheads	52,400	1,200	Adverse			
Administration overheads	32,420	4,580	Favourable			

Test 5

The following data is available about an organisation's costs and income in three months of 20X4:

- July: Variable costs £40,000, Fixed costs £15,000, Income £90,000

- August: Variable costs £35,000, Fixed costs £13,000, Income £42,000

- September: Variable costs £45,000, Fixed costs £18,000, Income £96,000

The organisation wishes to know:

(a) Its total costs in each month and for the quarter
(b) Its profit or loss is in each month and for the quarter

Prepare the following spreadsheet to calculate and present this data clearly:

	A	B	C	D	E	F
1						
2						
3						
4						
5						

Test 6

Data has been entered in the spreadsheet for the next three months. Show the formulae that you would use in each of the empty cells in the spreadsheet.

	A	B	C	D	E	F
1		Variable costs £	Fixed costs £	Total costs £	Income £	Profit/loss £
2	October	50,000	19,000		105,000	
3	November	59,000	14,000		94,000	
4	December	35,000	12,000		32,000	
5	Total for quarter					
	Average for quarter					

ANSWERS TO CHAPTER TASKS

CHAPTER 1   Introduction to basic costing systems

1

Transaction	Cash	Credit
Sale for £100		✓
Purchase of car	✓	

2

Activity	Yes
Analysing variances	
Decision-making	✓
Planning	✓
Selling goods and services	
Control	✓

CHAPTER 2   Elements of cost

1

Transaction	Capital	Revenue
Extension constructed onto a building	✓	
Repairs to a machine		✓
Depreciation charge on a vehicle		✓
Installation of new machinery	✓	
Redecorating offices		✓

2

Cost	Production cost	Selling and distribution cost	Administration cost
Factory rent	✓		
Managing Director's salary			✓
Sales Director's salary		✓	
Depreciation charge on office equipment			✓
Depreciation charge on plant and equipment	✓		
Fuel for delivery vans		✓	
Factory heating and lighting	✓		

3

	Direct cost	Indirect cost
Painter painting the building	✓	
Painter doing maintenance work in the toy factory		✓

This is a direct cost as the painter is working on the product directly. Painters doing maintenance work in a factory which makes toys would be classified as indirect labour. This emphasises the importance of considering each case on its own merits.

4

	£
Basic labour cost	395.60
Overtime labour cost	36.80

5

Cost centre	£
Vehicle deliveries	310
Motorbike deliveries	240
Bookings	600
Administration	600

CHAPTER 3   Cost behaviour

1

Output level (units)	Fixed cost per bench £
1,000	20
10,000	2
20,000	1
100,000	0.20

2

Description	Production cost centre	Service cost centre	Profit centre
Cutting, assembling, packing	✓		
Warehouse, stores, maintenance		✓	
Retail shop			✓

CHAPTER 4   Inventory classification and valuation

1

Characteristic	FIFO	LIFO	AVCO
Issues are valued at the most recent purchase cost		✓	
Inventory is valued at the most recent purchase cost	✓		
Issues are valued at the average of the cost of purchases			✓

CHAPTER 5   Classifying labour costs

1

	Direct cost £	Indirect cost £
Basic pay	370	
Overtime: basic	40	
Overtime: premium		20
Gross pay	410	20

2

Number of pockets	Gross pay £	Workings =
4,000	400.00	4,000 × 10p
500	60.00	500 × (10 +2)p
230	32.20	230 × (10 +2+2)p
Total	492.20	

We have included the workings here so you can see where the figures come from for the extra pockets sewn. You won't have to do workings in your answer for the real assessment unless you are asked to.

3

	Time-rate	Piecework rate
Easy to calculate an employee's pay	✓	
Can be used for all direct labour employees	✓	
More efficient workers are paid more than less efficient workers		✓
The quality of the goods produced is affected by workers rushing a job so that they earn more		✓
The employees' basic pay fluctuates if output fluctuates		✓
More supervisors may be needed for this system	✓	
Production problems can lead to a cut in pay		✓
Systems need to be set up to check the amount of work produced by each employee		✓

CHAPTER 6   Coding costs

1

	Cost £	Code
Pay at basic time-rate	395.60	010302
Overtime premium	36.80	010303
Employer's NIC	42.55	010303
Total cost	474.95	

2

INVOICE

Wilmshurst Furniture Makers
Retail Park
Dopham DR3 4ZJ

To: ┌ BOTS & CO ┐

Invoice number: 42118

Date/tax point: 5 Dec 20X6

Order number: PO 4662

└ ┘ **Account number:** SL 17

Quantity	Description	Inventory code	Unit amount £	Total £
6	Dining Chair	DC 08	56.00	021015 336.00
1	5ft Dining Table	DT 31	270.00	021011 270.00

Net total	606.00
VAT	121.20
Invoice total	727.20

Terms
Net 30 days
E & OE

3

Code	Opening balance £	Update £	Closing balance 31 Dec 20X6 £
021113	21,056	1,040	22,096
021116	96,100	960	97,060
021117	22,650	1,260	23,910
021212	53,682	310	53,992
021215	3,480	448	3,928
021219	12,420	520	12,940

CHAPTER 7   Comparison of costs and income

1

Profit centre	Actual income December 20X6 £	Budgeted income December 20X6 £	Variance £	Variance as % of budgeted income
Dopham	185,213	175,000	10,213 F	5.8
Nutley	167,232	170,000	2,768 A	1.6
Jenson	113,415	120,000	6,585 A	5.5

2   (a)   B5 =(B2+B3+B4)

C5 =(C2+C3+C4)

(b)   B5 =(B3*B4)

C5 =(C3*C4)

(c)   F2 =C2/B2

Answers to chapter tasks

TEST YOUR LEARNING – ANSWERS

CHAPTER 1   Introduction to basic costing systems

Test 1

Transaction	Cash	Credit
Purchase of a van with payment agreed in one month		✓
Sale of goods paid for by credit card	✓	
Purchase of printer cartridges accompanied by an invoice		✓
Sale of goods paid for by cheque	✓	
Purchase of printer cartridges by cheque	✓	

Test 2

	Capital	Revenue
Purchase of a computer for resale to a customer by a computer retailer		✓
Purchase of a computer by a computer retailer for use in the sales office	✓	
Payment of wages by an accounting firm		✓
Purchase of a building by a property developer to serve as head office	✓	

Test 3

	Statement of profit or loss	Statement of financial position
Sales revenue	✓	
Non-current assets		✓
Expenses	✓	
Current assets		✓
Profit or loss	✓	

Test 4

Characteristic	Financial accounting	Management accounting
It helps with decision-making within the business		✓
Its end-product consists of statements for external publication	✓	
It focuses on costs		✓
It focuses on asset valuations	✓	

CHAPTER 2   Elements of cost

Test 1

	£
Basic pay 38 hours @ £9.60	364.80
Overtime pay 3 hours @ 9.60 × 2	57.60
Total gross pay	422.40
Cost centres	
Baking – labour 15 hours @ £9.60	144.00
Throwing – labour (23 hours @ £9.60) + (3 hours @ £9.60 × 2)	278.40
Total labour cost	422.40

Test 2

Cost centre	£
Throwing – expense – rent £15,000 × 15%	2,250
Throwing – expense – cleaning	200
Throwing – Total	2,450
Baking – expense – rent £15,000 × 40%	6,000
Baking – expense – servicing	600
Baking – Total	6,600
Painting – expense – rent £15,000 × 15%	2,250
Packaging – expense – rent £5,000 × 20%	1,000
Stores – expense – rent £5,000 × 80%	4,000
Maintenance – expense – rent £15,000 × 10%	1,500
Selling and distribution – expense – rent £3,000 × 0.5	1,500
Selling and distribution – expense – advertising	400
Selling and distribution – Total	1,900
Canteen cost centre – expense – rent £15,000 × 20%	3,000
Administration – expense – rent £3,000 × 0.5	1,500

Test 3

Cost centre	£
Audit – consumables 489.00 × 30%	146.70
Tax – consumables 489.00 × 40%	195.60
Consultancy – consumables 489.00 × 20%	97.80
Administration – consumables 489.00 × 10%	48.90

Test 4

Cost	Materials	Labour	Expenses/overheads
Metal used for casing	✓		
Business rates on warehouse			✓
Wages of operatives in assembly department		✓	
Salary of factory supervisor			✓

Test 5

Cost	Direct	Indirect
Detergent used for cleaning floors	✓	
Depreciation of vacuum cleaner		✓
Wages of booking assistant		✓
Wages of cleaners	✓	

Test 6

Cost	Production	Administration	Selling and distribution
Purchases of sand	✓		
Fuel for salesperson's vehicle			✓
Printer paper for office		✓	
Wages of factory workers	✓		

CHAPTER 3   Cost behaviour

Test 1

(a)   **Fixed costs**

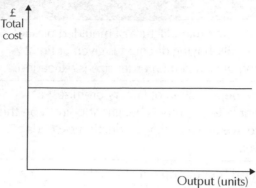

(b)   **Fixed cost per unit**

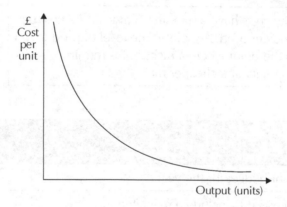

Test 2

	Cost behaviour fits the graph shape?
(a) Plastic used in the manufacture of moulded plastic furniture. A bulk-buying discount is given at Point A on the graph once a certain order size is exceeded.	No
(b) Straight-line depreciation of factory premises; a replacement larger factory is bought at point A on the graph once average monthly production exceeds a certain level.	Yes
(c) Rent of a warehouse. Additional warehouse space is rented at point A on the graph when inventory levels exceed a certain point.	Yes
(d) Electricity costs have a standing charge and a cost per unit of power used. At point A the level of production reaches the point where a nightshift is required, which uses electricity at a cheaper rate.	No

Test 3

Cost	Fixed	Variable	Semi-variable
Entertainment budget for the year	✓		
Telephone costs that include a fixed line rental charge plus call charges			✓
Leather used in the production process		✓	
Labour costs paid as production overtime		✓	

Test 4

	True	False
Total variable costs do not change directly with changes in activity but unit variable costs do		✓
Fixed costs per unit decrease with increasing levels of output	✓	
The semi-variable cost curve shows a step change when an element of cost suddenly increases in amount		✓

CHAPTER 4 Inventory classification and valuation

Test 1

	Raw materials	Part-finished goods	Finished goods
Bricks at a brick-making factory			✓
Bricks in stores at a building company	✓		
The ingredients for making bricks held in stores	✓		
A brick that has been moulded but not fired in the kiln		✓	

Test 2

(a) **FIFO**

Stores Ledger Account								
	Purchases			Sales			Balance	
Date	Quantity (kg)	Cost £	Total cost £	Quantity (kg)	Cost £	Total cost £	Quantity (kg)	Total cost £
3 Jan							100	880
16 Jan	400	9.00	3,600				500	4,480
27 Jan				100	8.80	880		
				150	9.00	1,350		
				250		2,230	250	2,250
5 Feb				180	9.00	1,620	70	630
9 Feb	400	9.30	3,720				470	4,350
17 Feb				70	9.00	630		
				350	9.30	3,255		
				420		3,885	50	465
25 Feb	500	9.35	4,675				550	5,140

Cost of material issues = £2,230 + £1,620 + £3,885

= £7,735

Value of closing inventory = £5,140

(b) **LIFO**

	Stores Ledger Account							
	Purchases			Sales			Balance	
Date	Quantity (kg)	Cost £	Total cost £	Quantity (kg)	Cost £	Total cost £	Quantity (kg)	Total cost £
3 Jan							100	880
16 Jan	400	9.00	3,600				500	4,480
27 Jan				250	9.00	2,250	250	2,230
5 Feb				150	9.00	1,350		
				30	8.80	264		
				180		1,614	70	616
9 Feb	400	9.30	3,720				470	4,336
17 Feb				400	9.30	3,720		
				20	8.80	176		
				420		3,896	50	440
25 Feb	500	9.35	4,675				550	5,115

Cost of material issues   = £2,250 + £1,614 + £3,896

                        = £7,760

Value of closing inventory   = £5,115

(c) **AVCO**

	Stores Ledger Account							
	Purchases			Sales			Balance	
Date	Quantity (kg)	Cost £	Total cost £	Quantity (kg)	Cost £	Total cost £	Quantity (kg)	Total cost £
3 Jan							100	880.00
16 Jan	400	9.00	3,600				500	4,480.00
27 Jan				250	8.96	2,240.00	250	2,240.00
5 Feb				180	8.96	1,612.80	70	627.20
9 Feb	400	9.30	3,720				470	4,347.20
17 Feb				420	9.25	3,885.00	50	462.20
25 Feb	500	9.35	4,675				550	5,137.20

Cost of material issues   = £2,240.00 + £1,612.80 + £3,885.00

                                  = £7,737.80

Value of closing inventory   = £5,137.20

Test 3

Characteristic	True	False
FIFO costs issues of inventory at the oldest purchase price	✓	
AVCO costs issues of inventory at the most recent purchase price		✓
LIFO costs issues of inventory at the most recent purchase price	✓	
FIFO values closing inventory at the oldest purchase price		✓
LIFO values closing inventory at the oldest purchase price	✓	
AVCO values closing inventory at an average purchase price	✓	

Test 4

Method	Cost of issue on 11 Oct	Closing inventory at 31 Oct
FIFO	£162.00	£958.00
LIFO	£202.50	£917.50
AVCO	£180.00	£940.00

CHAPTER 5   Classifying labour costs

Test 1

OPERATION CARD

Operator	Mary Dunnock	Works order No	1492
Clock No	16	Part No	233
Week ending	7.7.X6	Description	Wooden lids

Operation Sanding top and bottom surface using grade 2 sandpaper

Quantity produced	Quantity rejected	Good production	Rate £	£
Monday 350	12	338	0.14	47.32
Tuesday 428	21	407	0.14	56.98
Wednesday 483	2	481	0.14	67.34
Thursday 376	14	362	0.14	50.68
Friday 295	18	277	0.14	38.78

Employee number   352   Date   7.7.X6

Employee signature   MD

Supervisor's signature   S Ditford

Total gross pay   = £47.32 + £56.98 + £67.34 + £50.68 +£38.78

= £261.10

Test 2

	J Sparrow	K Finch	M Swallow	B Cuckoo
Total hours	39.5	37.5	38.75	37.5
Basic pay (35 × £7)	£245.00	£245.00	£245.00	£245.00
Time-and-a-half	(1.5 × £7 × 1.5)	(2.5 × £7 × 1.5)	(1.75 × £7 × 1.5)	(0.5 × £7 × 1.5)
	= £15.75	= £26.25	= £18.38	= £5.25
Double time	(3 × £7 × 2)		(2 × £7 × 2)	(2 × £7 × 2)
	= £42.00		= £28.00	= £28.00
Total gross pay	£302.75	£271.25	£291.38	£278.25

Test 3

Payment method	Time-rate	Time-rate plus bonus	Piecework	Differential piecework
Employees are paid for the hours worked and receive an incentive if a target is reached		✓		
Employees are paid for output achieved and receive an incentive as production increases				✓
Employees are paid only for output achieved			✓	
Employees are only paid for the hours worked	✓			

CHAPTER 6   Coding costs

Test 1

INVOICE

Purbeck Clay
Granite Yard
Compston BH3 4TL
Tel 01929 464810
VAT Reg 1164 2810 67

To: Pole Potteries

Invoice number: 36411

Date/tax point: 16 Dec 20X6

Order number: 11663

Account number: SL 42

Quantity	Description	Inventory code	Unit amount £	Total £
50 kg	Throwing clay	Tc412	6.80	111 340.00
10 litres	Paint - Fuchsia	Pf67	2.80	131 28.00
		Net total		368.00
		VAT		73.60
		Invoice total		441.60

Terms
Net 30 days
E & OE

INVOICE

IndCan Suppliers
High Street
Hamware BH3 7SP
Tel 01929 432432
VAT Reg 2214 6182 93

To: | Pole Potteries

Invoice number: 61212

Date/tax point: 17 Dec 20X6

Order number: 11668

Account number: PP 02

Quantity	Description	Inventory code	Unit amount £	Total £
100kg	Frozen chips	46112	1.20	181 120.00
48	Chicken pies	61297	0.90	181 43.20

Net total		163.20
VAT		32.64
Invoice total		195.84

Terms
Net 30 days
E & OE

Test 2

	£	Code
Throwing – labour 26 hours @ £9.60 =	249.60	112
Baking – labour 15 hours @ £9.60 =	144.00	122
Throwing – expense – overtime premium 3 × 9.60 =	28.80	113
Throwing – expense – employer's NIC	26.42	113
Baking – expense – employer's NIC	15.25	123

Test 3

	£	Code
Throwing – expense – rent £15,000 × 15%	2,250	
Throwing – expense – cleaning	200	
Throwing – total	2,450	113
Baking – expense – rent £15,000 × 40%	6,000	
Baking – expense – servicing	600	
Baking – total	6,600	123
Painting – expense – rent £15,000 × 15%	2,250	133
Packaging – expense – rent £5,000 × 20%	1,000	143
Stores – expense – rent £5,000 × 80%	4,000	153
Maintenance – expense – rent £15,000 × 10%	1,500	163
Selling and distribution – expense – rent £3,000 × 0.5	1,500	
Selling and distribution – expense – advertising	400	
Selling and distribution – total	1,900	173
Canteen – expense – rent £15,000 × 20%	3,000	183
Administration – expense – rent £3,000 × 0.5	1,500	193

Test 4

Transaction	Code
Materials for casings	2/10
Sales to Paris, EU	1/20
Business rates on factory	2/20
Sales commission paid	3/10
Sales to Holmfirth, UK	1/10
Office stationery	4/20

CHAPTER 7   Comparison of costs and income

Test 1

Comparison of November 20X6 cost centre costs with budget

	Actual £	Budget £	Variance £
Throwing			
Materials	12,140	11,200	940 A
Labour	7,440	6,150	1,290 A
Expenses	6,330	7,130	800 F
Baking			
Materials	1,330	1,500	170 F
Labour	2,440	2,490	50 F
Expenses	10,490	11,350	860 F
Painting			
Materials	4,260	3,660	600 A
Labour	13,570	11,240	2,330 A
Expenses	2,680	2,800	120 F

Cost centre	Expense	Variance £	Variance as a % of budget
Throwing	Materials	940 A	8.4
	Labour	1,290 A	21.0
	Expenses	800 F	11.2
Baking	Materials	170 F	11.3
	Labour	50 F	2.0
	Expenses	860 F	7.6
Painting	Materials	600 A	16.4
	Labour	2,330 A	20.7
	Expenses	120 F	4.3

Test 2

	True	False
The difference between a budgeted and an actual cost is called performance		✓
An adverse variance occurs when actual income exceeds budgeted income		✓

Test 3

Cost type	Budget £	Actual £	Variance £	Adverse	Favourable
Direct materials	52,480	51,940	540		✓
Direct labour	65,920	67,370	1,450	✓	
Production overheads	34,340	35,680	1,340	✓	
Selling and distribution overheads	10,270	12,840	2,570	✓	
Administration overheads	11,560	10,470	1,090		✓

Test 4

Cost type	Budget £	Variance £	Adverse/ Favourable	Variance as a % of budget	Significant	Not Signific
Direct materials	134,280	20,390	Favourable	15.2	✓	
Direct labour	128,410	5,400	Adverse	4.2		✓
Production overheads	87,360	9,280	Adverse	10.6	✓	
Selling and distribution overheads	52,400	1,200	Adverse	2.3		✓
Administration overheads	32,420	4,580	Favourable	14.1	✓	

Test 5

	A	B	C	D	E	F
1		Variable costs £	Fixed costs £	Total costs £	Income £	Profit/loss £
2	July	40,000	15,000	55,000	90,000	35,000
3	August	35,000	13,000	48,000	42,000	-6,000
4	September	45,000	18,000	63,000	96,000	33,000
5	Total for quarter	120,000	46,000	166,000	228,000	62,000

Test 6

	A	B	C	D	E	F
1		Variable costs £	Fixed costs £	Total costs £	Income £	Profit/loss £
2	October	50,000	19,000	=(B2+C2)	105,000	=(E2-D2)
3	November	59,000	14,000	=(B3+C3)	94,000	=(E3-D3)
4	December	35,000	12,000	=(B4+C4)	32,000	=(E4-C4)
5	Total for quarter	=SUM(B2:B4)	=SUM(C2:C4)	=SUM(D2:D4)	=SUM(E2:E4)	=SUM(F2:F4)
	Average for quarter	=AVERAGE (B2:B4)	=AVERAGE (C2:C4)	=AVERAGE (D2:D4)	=AVERAGE (E2:E4)	=AVERAGE (F2:F4)

INDEX

Notes

Notes

REVIEW FORM

How have you used this Text?
(Tick one box only)

☐ Home study

☐ On a course_____

☐ Other _____

Why did you decide to purchase this Text? *(Tick one box only)*

☐ Have used BPP Texts in the past

☐ Recommendation by friend/colleague

☐ Recommendation by a college lecturer

☐ Saw advertising

☐ Other _____

During the past six months do you recall seeing/receiving either of the following?
(Tick as many boxes as are relevant)

☐ Our advertisement in Accounting Technician

☐ Our Publishing Catalogue

Which (if any) aspects of our advertising do you think are useful?
(Tick as many boxes as are relevant)

☐ Prices and publication dates of new editions

☐ Information on Text content

☐ Details of our free online offering

☐ None of the above

Your ratings, comments and suggestions would be appreciated on the following areas of this Text.

	Very useful	Useful	Not useful
Introductory section	☐	☐	☐
Quality of explanations	☐	☐	☐
How it works	☐	☐	☐
Chapter tasks	☐	☐	☐
Chapter overviews	☐	☐	☐
Test your learning	☐	☐	☐
Index	☐	☐	☐

	Excellent	Good	Adequate	Poor
Overall opinion of this Text	☐	☐	☐	☐

Do you intend to continue using BPP Products?   ☐ Yes   ☐ No

Please note any further comments and suggestions/errors on the reverse of this page. You can e-mail your comments to ianblackmore@bpp.com.

Please return to: Ian Blackmore, AAT Product Manager, BPP Learning Media Ltd, FREEPOST, London, W12 8BR.

REVIEW FORM (continued)

TELL US WHAT YOU THINK

Please note any further comments and suggestions/errors below.